YOUR
AGENCY

YOUR AGENCY

Handle With Care

SPENCER J. CONDIE

Bookcraft
Salt Lake City, Utah

Library of Congress Catalog Card Number: 96-86083
ISBN 1-57008-286-3

First Printing, 1996

Printed in the United States of America

To devoted parents who never give up on their children.

To married couples with strong differences whose integrity to their marriage vows brings them to their knees each night in prayer.

To missionary companions who keep an eye "single to the glory of God" and strive hard to become as one.

To auxiliary presidencies, bishoprics and priesthood presidencies, and committees and councils who faithfully work to become united in a common cause.

To youth who have discovered their moral agency and inquisitively want to see how it works.

Know This, That Every Soul Is Free

Know this, that every soul is free
To choose his life and what he'll be;
For this eternal truth is giv'n:
That God will force no man to heav'n.

He'll call, persuade, direct aright,
And bless with wisdom, love, and light,
In nameless ways be good and kind,
But never force the human mind.

Hymns, no. 240

Contents

Acknowledgments . . . . *xi*

1 Is "Free Agency" Really Free? *1*

2 Beware of Chasing Parked Cars:
   The Enemies of Agency *11*

3 Culture and the Curse of Respectability *41*

4 War in Heaven and on Earth:
   But We Are Not Alone *61*

5 The Agency of Others: Handle with Care *85*

6 The Collective Convergence of Agency *109*

7 Yielding Our Hearts to God *133*

   Index *145*

Acknowledgments

I express deep gratitude to all the Brethren who have been my teachers and examples for the past several years. I honor and sustain them all as servants of the living God.

I am grateful to my daughters Stefanie and Heidi and my secretary, Karen B. Morgan, for their assistance in preparing the manuscript at various stages. The editors at Bookcraft have my sincere appreciation for their continual encouragement and assistance.

This book is not an official publication of The Church of Jesus Christ of Latter-day Saints. I alone am responsible for the views it expresses.

That every man may act in doctrine and principle . . .
according to the moral agency which I have given unto him,
that every man may be accountable for his own sins in the
day of judgment (D&C 101:78). ✒

Chapter One

Is "Free Agency" Really Free?

M any years ago I received a surprise visit from one of my former students at Brigham Young University. Such occasions are always a pleasant experience for any teacher, especially when the students have led happy, productive lives. This particular student was a very bright and lovely young woman who had excelled in her academic pursuits. Near the time of her graduation from the university she began seriously dating a young man from her home town. He was smitten with her and conveyed his intentions to marry her.

This young woman, whom we will call Diane, felt very unsure of herself with regard to his marriage proposal, so she sought the counsel of an elderly, trusted family friend. This kindly man had known her young suitor's family for several years, and he highly recommended the young man as a suitable husband for her. Based upon his enthusiastic recommendation she proceeded with the wedding plans.

About a year after their marriage she gave birth to a healthy young baby, but at the very time she should have been overwhelmingly happy she had come to the realization that her husband was emotionally immature, as evidenced by his uncontrollable outbursts of anger at the slightest provocation. Furthermore, he had neither ambition nor intention to accept the responsibility of supporting his new family. In a word, he was just plain lazy.

To keep food on the table, Diane juggled a job along with caring for her baby until she finally reached the point where a divorce seemed to be the only solution to her problems. As she recounted her troubles of the previous few years, I felt inclined to ask the question: "Diane, how do you feel toward the elderly family friend who counseled you to marry this young man?"

Her response indicated considerable spiritual maturity on her part. Said she: "I still admire and respect him as a valued friend. The mistake in judgment was mine. I went to him about a decision which *I* should have made. In essence, I handed him my agency when I should have accepted the responsibility myself. My elderly friend had known my husband *longer* than I had, but I knew him *better*, and I had information, experiences, and feelings which my friend did not have." Diane gained invaluable insight into herself and into the great plan of happiness when she discovered the pervasive importance of moral agency in her life.

President David O. McKay declared that "man's greatest endowment in mortal life is the power of choice—the divine gift of free agency. . . . Next to the bestowal of life itself, the right to direct that life is God's greatest gift. . . . [Men and women] may choose the right or they may choose the wrong. . . . But the Lord does not take from them their free agency." (*Gospel Ideals* [Salt Lake City: Improvement Era, 1953], pp. 299, 301.)

Notwithstanding the fact that the War in Heaven was fought over the issue of moral agency, among others, there are many people on the earth today who carelessly surrender their agency to others, and there are many other individuals who are always ready and willing to control the agency of others. Although there may be wisdom in seeking counsel from others, some troubled married couples seek to hand over their agency to priesthood leaders or professional family therapists as if dropping off a load of laundry at the dry cleaners expecting to pick it up two days later perfectly pressed with all the spots removed. Blessed with the power of discernment, bishops will provide wise counsel, but recommended changes in behavior and attitude are the responsibility of those who seek their counsel. Too many individuals go counselor shopping, seeking someone who will tell them exactly what to do and thus relieve them of the burden of exercising their agency.

Some young students base future career choices on flimsy information or upon an offhand comment by a favorite teacher. A casual comment by a mission president or a bishop is sometimes translated into a commandment by a young person selecting a future mate. There are reputable salesmen, counselors, and consultants in nearly every field imaginable who render a useful service, but our agency is too important to be handled casually and too sacred to be surrendered to someone else. We are accountable for the exercise of our agency; indeed, the Lord admonishes us to "be anxiously engaged in a good cause, and do many things of [our] own free will" (D&C 58:27).

Some therapists may advocate divorce, consultants might urge owners to sell their company, and sales personnel may advocate making a large purchase involving a client's life savings. All of these experts may think they have the best interests of their clients at heart, and the service they render may provide their respective clientele with valuable insights and information. In the final analysis, however, after seeking the counsel of others every individual has a responsibility to jealously guard his or her moral agency, assuming final accountability for decisions made.

The ubiquitous nature of agency is reflected in the following colloquial expressions in everyday life:

- Whatever your little heart desires.
- It's entirely up to you.
- It's your call.
- You have first choice.
- Have it your way.
- Would you like chocolate, vanilla, or strawberry?
- Your wish is my command.

Each of these foregoing expressions indicates a willingness of others to grant us wide latitude in the use of our personal agency.

Contrast the intent of those previous phrases with the following expressions:

- Mind your own business!
- You *always* have to have your own way.
- She just can't cut the apron strings.
- He is so domineering.
- They don't know the meaning of the word *compromise*.
- You'll do it because I said so!
- He is such a poor henpecked husband.
- She's such a browbeaten wife.
- Eat your spinach!

Implicit in each of these phrases is the notion of restricted agency, if not coercion. Every day of our lives *our* agency may be on a collision course with *someone else's* agency. How we avoid or reconcile such collisions is much of what the Lord's great plan of happiness is all about. As we learn to accommodate the agency of others through tolerance, persuasion, patience, long-suffering, compassion, and kindness, we gradually begin to acquire and nurture the traits of godliness required to regain the presence of our Heavenly Father and His Son.

The Premortal Council

When the plan of our Heavenly Father and Lucifer's proposed modifications to it were presented before the premortal council in heaven, the Father's plan was accepted with joy by the righteous spirits. The foundation of this plan was the principle of moral agency, the freedom to choose and to gain knowledge and experience in preparation for eventual godhood. President Ezra Taft Benson observed that "the right of choice . . .runs like a golden thread throughout the gospel plan" (*The Teachings of Ezra Taft Benson* [Salt Lake City: Bookcraft, 1988], p. 81). This gospel plan involved considerable risks, for with the freedom of choice comes the ability to make mistakes, to sin, to rebel, to disobey, and to transgress divine laws.

The Fall

A major difference between Latter-day Saint theology and the beliefs of most other Christian religions is the position of Adam and Eve in the eternal scheme of things. We recognize and revere Adam and Eve as the Lord's instruments in introducing freedom of choice into the world. Whereas much of the rest of Christianity views Adam and Eve as spiritual weaklings and the perpetrators of original sin, thanks to the Book of Mormon we have learned that "Adam fell that men might be; and men are, that they might have joy" (2 Nephi 2:25). We learn that "if Adam had not transgressed he would not have fallen, but he would have remained in the garden of Eden. And all things which were created must have remained in the same state in which they were after they were created; and they must have remained forever, and had no end." (2 Nephi 2:22.)

Furthermore, if Adam and Eve had not partaken of the fruit of the tree of knowledge of good and evil in the Garden of Eden "they would have had no children" (2 Nephi 2:23), the human race would have had no beginning, and the plan of salvation would have been thwarted in its very inception. Adam and Eve "would have remained in a state of innocence, having no joy, for they knew no misery; doing no good, for they knew no sin" (2 Nephi 2:23). Precisely because Adam and Eve were in a state of innocence before partaking of the forbidden fruit, we consider that action to be a transgression of a lesser law, done in order to fulfill the requirements of a greater law.

The gift of agency is a crucial and fundamental element of the plan of happiness, and agency can only be exercised when alternative choices are possible. Therefore, Lehi explained that "it must needs be, that there is an opposition in *all* things." Without such ubiquitous opposition "righteousness could not be brought to pass, neither wickedness, neither holiness nor misery, neither good nor bad." (2 Nephi 2:11; emphasis added.)

The fall of Adam provided the opportunity for goodness, righteousness, and holiness to be introduced into the world. Evil and the opportunity to sin were simultaneously introduced by the Fall as part and parcel of the gift of agency. Intertwined with the principle of agency was the principle of the Atonement, through which we could become cleansed from those sins and mistakes. Through our repentance and our participation in the essential ordinances of the gospel, through the atonement of Christ, we could become qualified to regain the presence of God. Jesus Christ accepted the Father's invitation to the question, "Whom shall I send?" (Abraham 3:27.) And it was He who would atone for our sins, if we would but repent and come unto Him.

Satan's proposal was rejected because in lieu of agency he promised to coerce all of our Father's children to be obedient "that one soul should not be lost" (Moses 4:1). This plan was one of no agency, no risk, no growth, and no eternal progression, yet he demanded the Father's honor for making such a proposal (see Moses 4:1). But there was an additional selfish flaw in Satan's plan. Because his plan allowed for no mistakes it required no atonement for sin, and thus he could save his own satanic skin from any suffering.

Satan and his followers have a reputation as sore losers, as evidenced by the fact that after the majority of spirits at the Grand Council indicated a desire to follow a plan based upon moral agency, Satan and his minions instigated a war in heaven in an attempt to impose their will upon others. During this great battle Satan's forces were overcome by Michael and his angels "by the blood of the Lamb, and by the word of their testimony" (Revelation 12:7–11). Satan and his followers were cast out of heaven "into the earth" (Revelation 12:9), and thus the war which began in heaven continues to rage here upon the earth. But the issues are still the same: coercion versus moral agency and the freedom of choice. And the participants from the initial war are basically the same. During the War in Heaven we had the home-court advantage of walking by sight. During the current battle away from home we must rely on faith, faith in the Lord Jesus Christ and faith in the power of His atoning sacrifice.

The Price of Agency

I am indebted to President Boyd K. Packer, who made us aware of the fact that the term *free agency* appears nowhere in holy writ. Instead, the scriptures generally speak of agency or free will, but when agency *is* modified it is referred to as *"moral* agency" (see D&C 101:78). Because the term *free agency* has been used so pervasively by various modern prophets, in this book I may on occasion use *free agency* and *moral agency* interchangeably, fully aware that the latter term is more correct.

Perhaps one reason for shying away from the term *free agency* is the fact that, in many aspects, free agency really is not free. To be sure, moral agency is a gift from our Father in Heaven inherent in the plan that He presented, we accepted, and the Savior fulfilled.

But in the sense that it was provided at a very high price, as the Apostle Paul taught the Corinthians, this great and wonderful plan of happiness is *not* free. "What? know ye not that your body is the temple of the Holy Ghost which is in you, which ye have of God, and ye are not your own? For ye are bought with a price." (1 Corinthians 6:19–20.)

That price, of course, was the atoning sacrifice of Jesus Christ, graphically described in His own words:

> For behold, I, God, have suffered these things for all, that they might not suffer if they would repent;
>
> But if they would not repent they must suffer even as I;
>
> Which suffering caused myself, even God, the greatest of all, to tremble because of pain, and to bleed at every pore, and to suffer both body and spirit—and would that I might not drink the bitter cup, and shrink—
>
> Nevertheless, glory be to the Father, and I partook and finished my preparations unto the children of men (D&C 19:16–19).

Every drop of that divine blood was shed in payment for an expensive plan that provided moral agency and the ability to sin, and, through the miracle of forgiveness, the opportunity to be cleansed from our sins through repentance, priesthood ordinances, and endurance to the end.

The Apostle Paul clearly forewarned us of the *price* of unwisely using our agency: "The wages of sin is death" (Romans 6:23). Each time we seriously misuse our moral agency and fail to repent, we suffer a penalty. By offending the Spirit we withdraw from His continual companionship; and if we persist in our deviant course of action we will experience the spiritual death spoken of by Paul. It has become readily apparent in recent years that when certain sins are committed, death may be physical as well as spiritual.

Alma taught that "wickedness never was happiness" (Alma 41:10), a reality more powerful than gravity. *Unhappiness is another price to be paid for misusing our agency.* To some of the recalcitrant generation of his day, Helaman explained, "Ye have sought for happiness in doing iniquity, which thing is contrary to the nature of that righteousness which is in our great and Eternal Head" (Helaman 13:38). The Prophet Joseph Smith taught that happiness is the design of our existence (see *Teachings of the Prophet Joseph Smith*, sel. Joseph Fielding Smith [Salt Lake City: Deseret Book Co., 1976], pp. 255–56). In light of the above teachings of Alma and Helaman, righteousness also ought to be the design of our existence.

Using our agency in making righteous choices also involves a price. The Savior's Sermon on the Mount has been described by President Harold B. Lee as "The Lord's Constitution for a Perfect Life" (*Decisions for Successful Living* [Salt Lake City: Deseret Book Co., 1973], pp. 54–62).

The Beatitudes may be viewed as a recipe for righteousness with incremental steps, beginning with "the poor in spirit who come unto [Christ]" (3 Nephi 12:3). The next step in the celestial direction is to *mourn*, especially for our sins, for "godly sorrow worketh repentance to salvation" (2 Corinthians 7:10). One then becomes meek and begins to hunger and thirst for righteousness. A natural sequel is a greater inclination to be merciful, an increased desire to become pure in heart, and a stronger desire to be a peacemaker (see 3 Nephi 12:5–9).

But even the proper and inspired use of our moral agency has a price indicated in the next beatitude: "And blessed are all they who are persecuted for my name's sake, for theirs is the kingdom of heaven" (3 Nephi 12:10). As we climb the steps outlined in the Beatitudes we soon humbly recognize that our lives are on a higher plane than those who love the things of this world. And notwithstanding our efforts to share with them gospel truths that can also elevate their lives, some of them will begin to persecute us and scoff at our way of life and point mocking fingers at those who have partaken of the fruits of the gospel (see 1 Nephi 8:26–27).

The Savior reserved a special blessing for those who would be reviled and persecuted and falsely accused for His sake: "Ye shall have great joy and be exceedingly glad, for great shall be your reward in heaven; for so persecuted they the prophets who were before you" (3 Nephi 12:11–12).

There is still another price attached to moral agency, and that includes the vicissitudes of life that we experience while enduring to the end. Much of the pain and discomfort we experience in life is not of our own making, the consequence of neither our sins nor our righteous deeds. Devoted parents lose an innocent child randomly killed in a drive-by shooting. A loving spouse is maimed for life in an accident caused by a drunken driver. An elderly married couple of modest means trust an unscrupulous investment counselor and lose their entire life's savings. All of these troubles were caused by the misused agency of others.

Of such apparent injustices, Elder Richard L. Evans said:

> Some of the ponderable problems, the unanswered questions, the seeming injustices and discrepancies and uncertainties . . . which we often have a difficult time in reconciling, will find answer and solution and satisfaction if we are patient and prayerful and willing to wait. Part of them are the price we pay for our free agency. We pay a great price for free agency in this world, but it is worth the price we pay. One of the cherished sentences I recall from the utterances of the Prophet Joseph Smith is that one which says that "an hour of virtuous liberty on earth is worth a whole eternity of bondage." So long as men have their free agency, there will be temporary injustices and discrepancies and some seemingly inexplicable things, which ultimately in our Father's own time and purpose will be reconciled and made right. (*Improvement Era*, June 1952, p. 435.)

The Savior's atonement bought us with a price. But whether we pay the price of repentance for our sins or the price of enduring persecution for our righteousness, any price we pay is only a token, partial payment, "for we know that it is by grace that we are saved, *after all we can do*" (2 Nephi 25:23; emphasis added).

Elder Russell M. Nelson has provided valuable insight into the exercise of our moral agency throughout our lives: "As you continue to face many challenging choices in life, remember, there is great protection when you know who you are, why you are here, and where you are going. Let your unique identity shape each decision you make on the path toward your eternal destiny. Accountability for your choices now will bear on all that lies ahead." ("Choices," *Ensign*, November 1990, p. 75.)

Moral agency is a God-given gift of inestimable, eternal worth and should be handled with great care.

Because that they are redeemed from the fall they have become free forever, knowing good from evil; to act for themselves and not be acted upon (2 Nephi 2:26). ❧

Chapter Two

Beware of Chasing Parked Cars: The Enemies of Agency

My good friend Elder William R. Bradford has a gift for turning a phrase which can be both profound and humorous. In describing certain individuals who are consumed by financial conquest and the ever-increasing consumption of goods, he said: "Some people are like dogs who are always chasing cars and don't know what to do once they've caught one." Then, with his typically broad smile he added: "A bulldog is nothing but a greyhound who couldn't break the habit of chasing parked cars."

On the pathway to perfection there are many attitudes and behaviors that, like parked cars, do nothing to bring us closer to our destination. Satan is a great master of deception who strives to lead each of us "*carefully* down to hell." (2 Nephi 28:21; emphasis added). Lucifer deceives us by gradually transforming love to lust, changing feelings of self-reliance to independence from Deity, gradually turning confidence into arrogance, and mutating meekness into discouragement.

Satan especially desires to derail the youth of the noble

birthright from the pathway to perfection. When our youth lose a testimony or surrender their moral agency, Satan robs them of the continual companionship of the Spirit precisely at the time when some of life's greatest decisions need to be made regarding missions, marriage, and future careers. Following are some factors that, like parked cars, may create the illusion of going somewhere but, in fact, prevent us from reaching our celestial goal.

Addiction

Viktor Frankl observed that "the Western world has solved the problem of survival. The struggle for survival is over. But the question of 'survival for what?' is still open." ("Forward," in Joseph B. Fabry, Reuven P. Bulka, and William S. Sahakian, eds., *Logotherapy in Action* [New York: Jason Aronson, Inc., 1979], p. ix.) Many people live in an "existential vacuum," leading empty lives completely devoid of purpose, meaning, and direction. Empty lives are akin to empty stomachs, and in impoverished countries where children go to bed hungry each night it is not uncommon for them to engage in geophagy, the practice of eating dirt. This is a desperate attempt to fill their stomachs and to provide their bodies with needed vitamins and minerals in the absence of anything more suitable.

Common dirt can temporarily fool the stomach into thinking it has received substantial nourishment. So it is with empty lives. An empty life without meaning must also be filled with something—almost anything. Some people fill their empty lives with endless hours of television, and many of them vicariously adopt the lives of soap opera characters. Others become addicted to alcohol, tobacco, gambling, pornography, and reading pulp magazines and tabloids. A recent addiction involves spending countless empty hours "chewing the fiber-optic fat" on the computer Internet with anonymous people in distant places (see Kendall Hamilton, Claudia Kalb, and Nina A. Biddle, "They Log On, But They Can't Log Off," *Newsweek*, December 18, 1995, pp. 60–61). Still others develop an unhealthy love affair with the refrigerator and totally disregard the proper care of their body temples.

Regardless of the specific addiction, addicts trade their moral agency for their favorite bad habit until it becomes no longer possible to choose what they will eat or drink or smoke or inject into their veins or how they will spend free time. Such people switch their decision-making capability to automatic pilot and lose hope of changing the direction of their lives. This is happening all across the United States. There is no real advantage to living in a free country if we are in bondage to negative personal habits.

Edward Luttwak, author of *The Endangered American Dream*, has voiced a concern with the emptiness of our interpersonal relationships in our mobile, urban society, especially relationships within extended kinship structures. He decries the fact that few of us even know who our second cousins are, and an increasing number of people have little contact with their first cousins. In some families even brothers and sisters feel no reciprocal obligations toward each other. In more recent years there has also been a precipitous decline in the corporate family. Loyalty toward one's employer is vanishing, and many companies provide their employees with little security. Luttwak contends that Americans compensate for their deficiencies through "therapeutic shopping," the habit of giving gifts to themselves, yet another form of addiction. (See "The National Prospect: A Symposium," in *Commentary*, November 1995, p. 80.)

Another widespread addiction throughout the Western world is Satan's smutty smorgasbord of pornography, now available in videos, magazines, television, movies, and the cyberspace Internet. In a general priesthood meeting President Gordon B. Hinckley shared the content of an anonymous letter from a thirty-five-year-old man who confessed to being absolutely addicted to pornography, an addiction he considered to be as strong and as real as addiction to alcohol or drugs. This young man wrote the following:

> I was first introduced to this material as a child. I was molested by an older male cousin and pornography was used to attract my interest. I am convinced that this exposure at an early age to sex and pornography is at the root of my addiction today. I think it is ironic that those who support the business of pornography say that it is a matter of freedom of expression. I have no freedom. I have lost my free agency because I have been unable to overcome this. It is a trap

for me, and I can't seem to get out of it. Please, please, please, plead with the brethren of the Church to not only avoid but eliminate the sources of pornographic material in their lives. . . .

Finally, President Hinckley, please pray for me and others in the Church who may be like me to have the courage and strength to overcome this terrible affliction. (As quoted in "Building Your Tabernacle," *Ensign*, November 1992, p. 51.)

Pornography is far more than a private, personal indiscretion. Having dealt with many marriages in difficulty over the years, I have found that pornography is not infrequently a contributing factor in disrupting marriage relationships. Before marriage a young suitor who is addicted to pornography during his courting days begins to look upon a woman not as an eternal companion and future mother to his children but as an object of physical gratification. After marriage, if the pornographic addiction continues, he begins to compare his wife to the sleazy models in the magazines, movies, or videos he reads or watches. Before long he has a tendency to view his wife as too pure, too refined, and too righteous as he makes demands upon her which would violate her moral agency, spiritual sensitivity, and sense of propriety. The Spirit withdraws from such a relationship and the couple are left to themselves to resolve their differences. So-called "private sins" are seldom private at all. When the light goes out in one person's life it dilutes his or her influence for good and subsequently impairs that person's relationship to everyone else.

During a stake conference I invited a silver-haired mother to explain to the Saints why she and her husband were so cheerful that particular Saturday evening. Both of them virtually glowed. This lovely sister explained that twenty-two years previously their then ten-year-old son had become rather innocently involved in experimenting with drugs and alcohol. When the boy was thirteen his parents became aware that he was an alcoholic.

For the next seventeen years their precious son lived a life of virtual hell on earth where his primary goal in life was to find the means to support his enslaving addictions. Each day his parents prayed and pleaded with the Lord to help them find the way to recover this lost soul. After an absence of seventeen years, one day his parents reached him by telephone and invited him to come back home—and he did. This young prodigal confessed that on the day of the phone call he had fully intended to take his own life as an escape from his ever-increasing misery. His loving parents enrolled him in a therapeutic program that helped rid him of his enslaving addiction.

Two years had now passed, and why were these parents so extremely happy? In two weeks they would accompany their son to the holy temple, where he would worthily receive his sacred endowment. I was privileged to go through the temple with this fine young man and his loved ones on that spiritual occasion, and that day there was a little corner of heaven here on earth.

A few years ago I was seated in the airport in Copenhagen awaiting my flight to our home in Frankfurt. Seated immediately behind me was an elderly couple from Iowa who had obviously just completed one of those European tours that includes thirty cities in thirty days. This couple spoke quite loudly, so it was very easy to overhear their conversation, which unfolded approximately as follows:

"Well, Harvey, we finally made it. This has been the fastest month of my entire life."

"Yeah, Mildred, it sure has, and it's been the hardest month, too," Harvey said in agreement.

Mildred continued: "I want you to know how much I appreciate your carryin' around that heavy box of Dutch porcelain dishes we bought our very first day in Amsterdam."

Harvey replied: "That's been a real hassle draggin' 'em through every bus station and train station and airport, not to mention anything about tryin' to get 'em through Customs in each country."

"Well, I do love you for it, dear," Mildred said consolingly.

Then there was a long lull in the conversation. Finally, Mildred broke the silence. "Harvey, I've been thinkin'. You know at home we got the Melmac and the stoneware and the china dishes in the cupboard. Where we gonna put these new Dutch porcelain dishes?"

"Yeah," Harvey said, "I've been wonderin' about that too."

There was another long pause. Suddenly Harvey sat upright and said: "Maybe the dang things'll get broke on the plane and then we won't have to worry about 'em." Sensing the irony of their predicament, both Mildred and Harvey began to laugh uncontrollably.

Much of the happiness or misery we experience in our lives is the result of the habits, the friends, and the experiences we have gained and retained throughout our journey here on earth. But the time will come in each of our lives when we must pass through celestial Customs, and the material possessions we have accumulated for so long simply cannot be taken into the celestial kingdom.

Today is a good day to begin taking inventory of those possessions and personality traits and characteristics we wish to retain and those we wish to jettison. Mildred and Harvey made the connection rather late in their trip that certain goods of this world are more burdensome than helpful. Surely the accumulation of things has little connection with true happiness.

Debt

The accumulation of financial debt is another dangerous incursion upon our moral agency. A poignant description of the destructive power of debt was provided by President J. Reuben Clark:

> Interest never sleeps nor sickens nor dies; it never goes to the hospital; it works on Sundays and holidays; it never takes a vacation . . . it has no love, no sympathy; it is as hard and soulless as a granite cliff. Once in debt, interest is your companion every minute of the day and night; you cannot shun it or slip away from it; you cannot dismiss it; it yields neither to entreaties, demands, or orders; and whenever you get in its way or cross its course or fail to meet its demands, it crushes you. (In Conference Report, 6 April 1938, p. 103.)

The quest to find happiness and contentment through the acquisition of earthly possessions will ultimately fail. We should avoid debt like the plague. It is always wise to pay as we go. Unnecessary indebtedness in some families may overpower the moral agency of its members. In order to service an inordinately high monthly mortgage payment, a wife and mother seemingly has no other choice but to leave the home for outside employment. The husband and father may have to work at two jobs, including one on Sunday, in order to make ends meet. Time together as a family disappears as each of its members pays more homage to their house than to their home.

There are, of course, justifiable occasions when one incurs debt, such as for the purchase of a house or a major business investment. But the house need be no larger than is really necessary, and the business investment should be based upon sound financial information and not a wild-eyed get-rich-quick scheme.

All too frequently debt is accumulated unnecessarily, primarily in an attempt to keep up with the Joneses. Not only does such debt put *us* in bondage, but it also places undue pressure on the Joneses. Mary Ellen Edmunds observed that "we spend money that we don't have for things we don't need to impress people we don't like." (*Provo [Utah] Daily Herald*, November 22, 1995, p. B1).

The lines of William Wordsworth have more relevance today even than in a previous century when he penned them:

> The world is too much with us; late and soon
> Getting and spending, we lay waste our powers.

Sometimes we do not realize how much our materialistic world does, indeed, lay waste our powers until we step out of this sensate Western society into the Third World, as do those who serve a mission or visit another part of the world where three meals a day constitute a luxury. A missionary couple who returned from the Philippines shared the observation that "we had no idea how much we could do without and still be extremely happy."

Another missionary couple, who had lived in India, reported that one wise yet economically impoverished man told them: "In America you have much wealth, but your families are very poor. In our country we are very poor, but our families are very rich, indeed."

Discouragement

Another stalled car along life's highway is discouragement. Discouragement and its fellow travelers, despair and hopelessness, are much like the proverbial rocking chair: they keep us busily occupied, but they do not take us anywhere.

When I was but a young lad a new invention called television was beginning to sweep the country. I recall going to a friend's house to view my first World Series game between the Brooklyn Dodgers and the New York Yankees on a 14-inch screen in black-and-white, and thinking I had beheld a modern miracle. After the game a friend and I went to an electrical appliance store to investigate the cost of a television set. My friend asked the salesman what the difference was between a 14-inch TV and a 21-inch TV. With a very straight face the salesman replied: "With a 14-inch TV you mostly just see the infield or the pitcher's mound and the batter's box, but with a 21-inch TV you can see the whole ballpark!"

That settled it. I went home to inform my parents that when we bought a television set it absolutely had to be of the 21-inch variety, because I wanted to see the whole ballpark.

Discouragement is much like a shrinking television screen. Our view of the world becomes smaller and smaller until we can only see ourselves and our seemingly overwhelming problems. As we wallow in discouragement we lose the big picture of the great plan of happiness. Soon we lose all vestiges of self-confidence; and as we lose confidence in our ability to overcome our problems our moral agency starts to shrink, and we begin to view life in terms of very limited options and very little hope for success. But each time we overcome an obstacle in our lives we gain greater confidence and increased ability to surmount the next wave of opposition. Like Joseph Smith in the Liberty Jail, we need to be reminded that all our tribulations "shall give [us] experience, and shall be for [our] good." We should also remember that "the Son of Man hath descended below them all" and ask the introspective question, Am I "greater than he?" (D&C 122:7–8.)

In the previous section the Lord supplies a foolproof formula for regaining both comfort and confidence:

> Let thy bowels also be full of charity towards all men, and to the household of faith, and let virtue garnish thy thoughts unceasingly; then shall thy confidence wax strong in the presence of God; and the doctrine of the priesthood shall distil upon thy soul as the dews from heaven.
>
> The Holy Ghost shall be thy constant companion, and thy

scepter an unchanging scepter of righteousness and truth; and thy dominion shall be an everlasting dominion, and without compulsory means it shall flow unto thee forever and ever. (D&C 121: 45–46.)

Several years ago I received two heart-tugging letters on the same day. The first one I opened was written by a single woman in her mid-thirties. She described in detail the loneliness and lack of fulfillment she felt in her life, and she wondered if Heavenly Father had forgotten her.

The second letter was written by a married woman, also in her mid-thirties. She had graduated from college, served a mission, and married in the temple, and she was now the mother of four children. But her storybook ending did not contain much of "happily ever after." She explained that her husband was emotionally immature and had an extremely volatile temper. He had had eleven different jobs during the past six years. Each time his employer or supervisor would criticize his work he would immediately throw a temper tantrum and quit his job on the spot. This mother of four little ones explained how difficult it was to make ends meet when her husband's employment was always on the margin.

For a fleeting moment I had an overwhelming urge to send the single woman's letter to the married woman and the married woman's letter to the single woman. The one was discouraged about being single while the other was discouraged about being married. But the great plan of happiness is based upon the principle of moral agency, which requires an opposition in *all* things. While we may not be able to immediately alter our present circumstances, internally each of us has the personal power and ability to alter our attitudes toward our lot in life, to reach out to others, and to claim the blessings that come from losing ourselves in the service of others.

When I was a boy of about ten, I went to a carnival held in conjunction with the annual summer rodeo in my hometown. My cousin Keith and I decided to ride the Ferris wheel together. He would have been six or seven years old at the time, and he has always been known for his delightful laughter. I have enjoyed many Ferris wheel rides throughout the years, but what made this particular ride memorable was the fact that it lasted so long.

While we were standing in line waiting our turn, we observed that the Ferris wheel operator took about five minutes to load up the sixteen seats, and after that the large wheel made only about eight rotations before starting to unload the passengers again. But on this particular warm summer evening the brake mechanism suddenly failed, making it impossible for the operator to end our journey. After about the fifteenth revolution Keith and I realized that this was our lucky day.

Each time we passed the frustrated operator, who was struggling to repair his brakes, Keith would giggle uncontrollably. In retrospect, I do not know what delighted me more, the thrill of an unlimited ride or the joy experienced by my younger cousin.

In the seat behind us sat a young girl aged about seven who viewed this experience through anxious eyes. When she first realized the Ferris wheel was running out of control she began to shout her objections and demanded to get off, but with each successive revolution her apprehension increased from subdued sobbing to almost hysterical shrieking. What was a fine form of entertainment for us had become a source of terror for her.

Three decades later when I was a mission president, I shared the parable of the Ferris wheel with a young man who had concluded that, due to his incurable homesickness, it was time for him to go home early. I likened his mission to that runaway Ferris wheel ride—once aboard, he could either enjoy the ride immensely or he could be miserable the entire time, but he had been called by the prophet of God to serve for two full years. This fine young man caught the spirit of the modern parable and decided he would stay aboard for the entire ride. I am pleased to report that he endured to the end having served an honorable mission.

I have found through personal experience that whenever I am discouraged and start thinking only of myself and how hard hit I have been, if I kneel in prayer and count my many blessings I come to realize that I am truly blessed above most people on the face of the earth. When I pray for the suffering little children in Bosnia-Herzegovina, in Somalia, Rwanda, Burundi, and Haiti, all of a sudden my problems shrink to almost nil.

As my personal problems dissolve, my panoramic vision of this wonderful world and the great plan of happiness begins to expand

and I feel much closer to my Heavenly Father, to the Savior, to the Comforter, to my family, and to all those around me.

At the conclusion of the fourteen-year war (74 to 61 B.C.) between the Lamanites and the Nephites, "because of the exceedingly great length of the war between the Nephites and the Lamanites many had become hardened, and many were softened because of their afflictions, insomuch that they did humble themselves before God, even in the depth of humility" (Alma 62:41).

Participants in that great war had all suffered similar deprivations and hardships. The terror of war had impacted them more or less equally. But from this same experience, some of the people "had become hardened" while many others were "softened because of their afflictions." We may not be able to change our current circumstances, our failing health, our economic challenges, our loneliness from being apart from loved ones, but we can employ our moral agency to change our attitude toward those circumstances and toward the future. There are many, many avenues to joy and fulfillment within the constraints of our immediate environment, and one of the most productive courses of action is to forget ourselves and begin serving others.

Faith, hope, and charity are godly attributes which, when acquired and accompanied by participation in essential ordinances, will help to qualify us for entrance into the celestial kingdom some day. But in addition these attributes have urgent relevance in helping us to fend off the fiery darts of the adversary in today's world. Faith and hope are antidotes for discouragement, depression, and despair, and charity immunizes us against paranoia and acute high blood pressure, ulcers, and migraine headaches in the wake of offensive behavior by others.

Arrogance

During the Savior's earthly ministry He demonstrated great compassion toward the weak and infirm, the leprous, and those who were blind or deaf, halt or lame. He also showed great mercy toward sinners, declaring that "they that be whole need not a physician" (Matthew 9:12). But one group He could not abide was that of the arrogant, self-serving scribes and Pharisees, who "outwardly appear righteous unto men, but within . . . are full of hypocrisy and iniquity" (Matthew 23:28).

When Korihor, the anti-Christ, sought to undermine the faith of the ancient Nephites at the time of Alma's ministry, he articulated a doctrine of arrogance. Striking at the very heart of the gospel, the atonement of Christ, Korihor claimed that "there could be no atonement made for the sins of men, but every man fared in this life according to the management of the creature; therefore every man prospered according to his genius, and that every man conquered according to his strength; and whatsoever a man did was no crime" (Alma 30:17).

Arrogance generates a sense of independence from our Heavenly Father as self-made men begin to worship their creator. Such pride is completely alien to gratitude, one of the indispensible attributes of godliness (see D&C 59:21). We severely limit our moral agency when our pride excludes the alternative of calling down the powers of heaven to help us in our personal lives. The right kind of learning can expand important vistas in our lives, but the arrogant think they already know all that needs to be known. To such as these, G. K. Chesterton observed, "How much larger your life would be if your self could become smaller in it" (*Orthodoxy* [New York: Doubleday, 1990], p. 20).

The Lord has admonished us, "As all have not faith, seek ye diligently and teach one another words of wisdom; yea, seek ye out of the best books words of wisdom; seek learning, even by study and also by faith" (D&C 88:118). Somewhat later He revealed that "whatever principle of intelligence we attain unto in this life, it will rise with us in the resurrection. And if a person gains more knowledge and intelligence in this life through his diligence and obedience than another, he will have so much the advantage in the world to come." (D&C 130:18–19.)

Elaborating upon the Lord's revelation on learning, Elder Neal A. Maxwell contends that "for a disciple of Jesus Christ, academic scholarship is a form of worship. It is actually another dimension of consecration. Hence one who seeks to be a disciple-scholar will take both scholarship and discipleship seriously; and, likewise, gospel covenants. For the disciple-scholar, the first and second great commandments frame and prioritize life. How else could one worship God with all of one's heart, might, *mind*, and strength? (Luke 10:27.)" ("The Disciple-Scholar," in Henry B. Eyring, ed., *On Becoming a Disciple-Scholar* [Salt Lake City: Bookcraft, 1995], p. 7; emphasis in original.)

Notwithstanding the scriptural injunctions to improve our minds and increase our learning and knowledge, the Lord also gave us a timeless warning:

> O that cunning plan of the evil one! O the vainness, and the frailties, and the foolishness of men! When they are learned they think they are wise, and they hearken not unto the counsel of God, for they set it aside, supposing they know of themselves, wherefore, their wisdom is foolishness and it profiteth them not. And they shall perish.
>
> But to be learned is good if they hearken unto the counsels of God. (2 Nephi 9:28–29.)

Advanced degrees from institutions of higher learning can become a great blessing to ourselves and to others when we apply our knowledge to alleviating human suffering, to improving the quality of life, or to edifying the human spirit through the creation of great literature, music, or other fine arts. But when our much learning of secular knowledge becomes a substitute for the sacred knowledge that matters most, and when our university degrees become the only measurement of our worth as individuals, our much learning can become a stalled car on the road to perfection. One old sage observed: "You can always tell a Ph.D., but ya can't tell 'em much."

Education has a great potential for helping to maximize our moral agency as we become aware of an ever-increasing number of choices in our lives. But education can also become a restricting force in our lives if the "well-educated" become slavish adherents to the philosophies of men that run counter to the liberating truths of the restored gospel.

I am greatly impressed with how unimpressed the General Authorities of the Church are with each other's worldly credentials. Often their previous education and training serves them well in their current callings, but their greatest talents are their teachableness and their ability to listen to the promptings of the Spirit and to follow the prophet.

Rumor

After the War in Heaven was transferred to earth, Satan and his minions began using many of the same strategies in their war for the souls of men as were used by mortal military men in waging war. One of these strategies has been guerrilla warfare, a Spanish term meaning "little war." After conquering much of western Europe, Napoleon attempted to overcome the Iberian Peninsula between 1808 and 1813. The Spanish knew that their armies were no match for the well-trained and far more numerous French troops; but the Spaniards were much better acquainted with the rugged terrain of the mountainous Pyrenees region. Through stealth and hit-and-run surprise attacks the much smaller band of Spaniards instigated guerilla warfare and were successful in foiling the French attempt to conquer Spain. Eventually, Napoleon turned to easier areas of conquest.

In an attempt to deprive us of our moral agency, Satan also successfully uses guerilla warfare in our personal lives. Just before the Savior's birth in Bethlehem, half a world away the inhabitants of ancient America were being buffeted by Satan as he attempted to undermine the faith of the people at the very time Jesus came into the world. We read in the book of Helaman that the people imagined in their hearts many things "which were foolish and vain; and they were much disturbed, for Satan did stir them up to do iniquity continually; yea, he did go about *spreading rumors* and contentions upon all the face of the land, that he might harden the hearts of the people against that which was good and against that which should come" (Helaman 16:22; emphasis added).

The spiritually debilitating influence of rumor can be one of Satan's most insidious hit-and-run tactics that can critically curtail another's moral agency. An unidentified author aptly described the consequences of gossip, the identical twin of rumor:

Gossip

My name is Gossip.
I have no respect for justice.
I maim without killing.
I break hearts and ruin lives.
I am cunning and malicious and gather strength with age.
The more I am quoted, the more I am believed.
I flourish at every level of society.
My victims are helpless.
They cannot protect themselves against me because I have
    no name and no face.
To track me down is impossible.
The harder you try, the more elusive I become.
I am nobody's friend.
Once I tarnish a reputation, it is never quite the same.
My name is Gossip.

During the early days of the restored Church, apostate enemies of the Church became Satan's instruments in undermining the faith of the newly converted Saints through spreading malicious rumors about various leaders of the Church. During the dedicatory prayer of the Kirtland Temple, the Prophet Joseph Smith implored the Lord "to bring to shame and confusion, all those who have spread lying reports abroad, over the world, against thy servant or servants" (D&C 109:29).

To a lesser extent that practice continues today in some corners of the world. Hugh Nibley once remarked that "a shabby substitute for repentance is to compare our life with someone wickeder than we are." Rumormongers and those who thrive on gossip engage in just such a practice. By tarnishing the reputation of others, they fancy that their own reputation increases in brightness.

Rumor too often becomes a satanic substitute for reconciliation, but the Lord's conciliatory pattern is described in detail in the Doctrine and Covenants:

> And if thy brother or sister offend thee, thou shalt take him or her between him or her and thee *alone*; and if he or she confess thou shalt be reconciled.

And if he or she confess not thou shalt deliver him or her up unto the church, not to the members, but to the elders. And it shall be done in a meeting, and that not before the world.

And if thy brother or sister offend many, he or she shall be chastened before many. (D&C 42:88–90; emphasis added.)

Rumors can destroy one's credibility and bring about financial ruin as the integrity of a businessman, a physician, an attorney, or an educator is called into serious question. But notwithstanding the debilitating impact of gossip in eroding, at least temporarily, the latitude of our moral agency, we can take heart from the lives of great men who rose above the false accusations of others. In the twilight of his life, Herbert Hoover was asked how he handled all the critics and detractors who laid the fault of the Great Depression at his feet while he was serving as the president of the United States. Said President Hoover, with a twinkle in his eye: "I simply outlived all of those rascals."

Although the Prophet Joseph Smith was falsely accused on numerous occasions, he stayed the course with "an eye single to the glory of God" (D&C 4:5) and with each passing decade his stature as the Prophet of the Restoration has fulfilled the prophecy that "the ends of the earth shall inquire after thy name" (D&C 122:1).

An Unforgiving Heart

Another insidious form of satanic guerilla warfare is the holding of grudges, a private, ongoing skirmish, usually with one other person, which stops short of full-fledged war. One of the most ungodly attributes anyone can possess is the tendency to hold grudges. The Lord revealed that "my disciples, in days of old, sought occasion against one another and forgave not one another in their hearts" (D&C 64:8).

One may be inclined to ask: But how does an unforgiving heart severely limit our agency? Whenever we hold a grudge against another, our social life becomes akin to walking through a rattlesnake-infested wilderness. We are always afraid we might accidentally encounter our enemy, and this fear robs us of much of the joy in our life. If we go to a church meeting, the temple, the shopping mall, a ball game, or a concert, we must be ever vigilant to avoid a chance meeting with the person we cannot forgive. I have known a few folks with such carefully cultivated grudges that the mere sight of a particular person caused their faces to flush, their stomachs to churn, their pulse to quicken, and their blood pressure to become elevated to dangerously high levels.

Two common characteristics of professional grudge-holders are long memories and a penchant for making long lists. They carefully catalogue each and every offense for continuous future reference. Kai Erikson described this phenomenon in individuals who have experienced traumatic events in their lives: "Trauma has the quality of converting that one sharp stab into an enduring state of mind. A chronicler of passing events may report that the episode itself lasted no more than an instant—a gunshot, say—but the traumatized mind holds on to that moment, preventing it from slipping back into its proper chronological place in the past, and relives it over and over again in the compulsive musings of the day and the seething dreams of night. The moment becomes a season; the event becomes a condition." (Kai Erikson, *A New Species of Trouble: Explorations in Disaster, Trauma, and Community* [New York: W. W. Norton, 1994], p. 230.)

It is also common for those with unforgiving hearts to add to their own personal list of offenses and offenders those who have offended their friends and family members. In doing so they become self-appointed guardians of injustice in the world. Grudges become contagious, and like a metastasized cancer they begin to spread, as evidenced by the legendary feud between the Hatfield and McCoy clans, whose extended families perpetuated the family feud throughout each succeeding generation. Such grudges restrict our agency in a wide spectrum of life's activities. We are not free to buy a particular kind of automobile because the Hatfields are the car dealers. Our children cannot go to certain school activities because the McCoy children are in charge. And on and on it goes until the only purpose to one's life becomes doing battle with the enemy.

But the Lord has provided a prescription against grudges: "Wherefore, I say unto you, that ye ought to forgive one another; for he that forgiveth not his brother his trespasses standeth con-

demned before the Lord; for there remaineth in him the greater sin.
I, the Lord, will forgive whom I will forgive, but of you it is required
to forgive all men." (D&C 64:9–10.)

Does this scriptural injunction mean that we must forgive a
neighbor whose dog has just dug up our freshly planted garden? Yes!
Are children who were harshly disciplined by insensitive parents
required to forgive them? Yes! Must parents forgive a wayward child
who has brought dishonor to their family? Yes! Must we forgive a
friend who violated our trust and deceived us into losing our life's
savings? Yes! Must we forgive a bishop or stake president who failed
to properly release us from a Church calling? Yes! And do these
verses require husbands and wives to forgive each other, even if
infidelity is involved? Yes! (The actual resolution of family problems involving infidelity or severe abuse may lead to the dissolution
of a marriage, but even then all parties are required to forgive one
another.)

All of us have had numerous occasions when others have either
intentionally or unintentionally offended us, and the human inclination is to continually maintain a list of grievances as growing
proof that others do not truly value our human worth. I can relate
to those feelings. When I was in my teens I sometimes helped my
mother scrub the kitchen floor. One Saturday morning as we were
on our knees together, Mother, well known for her candor, said:
"Son, you're now old enough to know the truth—you're not very
good-looking. I don't want you to go through high school conceit-
ed and thinking you're the answer to every girl's prayers."

Well, I knew my mother loved me, so I shrugged off her observation without too much lingering damage to my self-esteem. I
went on a mission, graduated from college, got married and was
much relieved that a wife so beautiful would even consider being
seen with me in public.

Following graduate school I joined the faculty of Brigham
Young University, and shortly thereafter a friend from high school
days, who was working for the BYU Motion Picture Studio, called
to invite me to be involved in a filmstrip they were producing on
time management. Always wanting to be helpful, I cheerfully
acceded to his request and showed up at the studio for a recording
and photography session. I was to play the role of an extremely busy

young bishop, and one of my lines was: "There are so many things I have to do, I just can't seem to find the time to get them all done." They recorded my lines several times to assure they had a good recording, and then they told me thanks and said good-bye.

I asked, "But when do we do the photography?"

The producer of the filmstrip indicated that the photography takes place separately, a few weeks after they have edited the audio recordings.

I returned to my office and waited for the phone to ring informing me that I was to return to the studio to be photographed in various scenes accompanying the recorded script. The phone call never came.

Some time later I was invited to a large meeting of Saints where it was explained that a recently produced filmstrip on time management would be shown. Sure enough, here was the premiere showing of the filmstrip in which I had participated. As the filmstrip progressed, we observed a tall, dark, and handsome bishop who said in a voice very familiar to me: "There are so many things I have to do, I just can't seem to find the time to get them all done." I thought to myself: "Those unscrupulous knaves agree with my mother—they'll use my voice, but not my face."

The years rolled by, and one Saturday afternoon I went to a football game with my young son. It was a drizzly afternoon, so we took a couple of rubberized ponchos with us to keep dry. We looked very much like a couple of male Little Red Riding Hoods. The game had been televised live that afternoon, and as soon as we returned home our son's older sisters exclaimed: "Craig, we saw you on TV. The camera was focused on the field, and then suddenly they zoomed into the spectators in the bleachers, and your face filled the whole screen, and you looked so-o-o cute in your poncho."

I asked them, "Girls, how did *I* look?"

"We didn't see *you*, Dad," they replied.

"But you *had* to," I protested, "because I was sitting right next to Craig."

"Sorry, Dad," they said consolingly, "but we only saw Craig on TV."

Once again, I had been overlooked because of my looks.

A few years later I was called to serve as a General Authority along with eleven other men. A photographer from the *Ensign* magazine took a group photograph that later appeared on page 37 of the May 1989 issue of the *Ensign*. The caption under the photo reads: "Some of the members of the First and Second Quorums of the Seventy, including twelve new members." But there are not twelve newly called Seventies in the picture. There are *eleven* faces and one left ear. And that left ear belongs to me.

We were then sent to Europe, where I initially served as second counselor to Elder Carlos Asay. While visiting one of the districts in Spain, I learned that there had been some dissension in the ranks because some of the members felt their branch president or district president did not fully appreciate them and had not adequately thanked them for their service while extending a release to them. I shared with the Saints my experience of not being included in the photo of the twelve newly called Seventies, and told them we have to rise above such petty offenses.

After the meeting the district president, a very jovial fellow, asked if someone could take a photo with me in the center, the mission president on my right, and he himself on my left. A couple of weeks later I received a copy of the photo with a little note: "Dear President Asay, we finally got both of your ears in the picture." Once again, I had been offended—he did not even know my name!

But my little saga of ongoing persecution is trivial indeed as compared to the plight of those whose lives have been permanently scarred by the careless actions of others. One such person is Marty Doumas of Manhattan, Montana. Marty used to operate a Caterpillar bulldozer at the county landfill. On August 24, 1994, a U.S. Customs Service inspector brought 3,670 pounds of highly inflammable fireworks to the landfill, instructing Marty to spread them thinly across the landfill and then to crush and bury them.

As Marty was backing up, there was a tremendous explosion and he was suddenly enveloped in flames. His skin was charred, some of it hanging from his arms, and his watch had half melted. Marty later said: "I've never felt any anger toward anyone. I never felt 'Why me?'" Notwithstanding the extremely painful multiple skin grafts he has undergone, Marty explained: "I'm thankful it happened to me instead of anybody else. It could have happened to two or three people who worked at the landfill, who had young families. I could handle it better than them, I think. I just consider it an accident. It's nobody's fault. . . . I don't believe in lawsuits. If I can't get complete mobility, it might be fair to get a settlement. But I'm not looking to retire off the accident."

Marty's wife added: "I guess my philosophy is, when something happens, it's over and done with and has to be dealt with." (Gail Schontzler, "Victim of Horrible Burns Is at Peace, Gives Thanks," *Provo [Utah] Daily Herald*, November 24, 1994, p. B13.)

Another hero with a forgiving heart is former New York City police officer Steven McDonald. On the afternoon of July 7, 1986, the twenty-nine-year-old officer stopped a few young boys for questioning about some suspicious behavior. Suddenly a shot rang out and officer McDonald slumped to the ground. A bullet had severed his spinal cord, leaving him paralyzed from the chin down. The culprit was Shavod Jones, a boy of fifteen, who had been previously convicted of armed robbery.

Recalling the events of that fateful day, McDonald said: "When I was shot, I was dying, and my family and I said all sorts of prayers. I wanted to be forgiven then for my sins, and if I was to be forgiven by God, I had to forgive Shavod Jones." He added: "I feel God's love more now than I'd ever felt it in my life. . . . My forgiving Shavod has had a powerful effect." McDonald now spends much of his time speaking to various groups, including schoolchildren, about the importance of forgiving those who have harmed us. (Rick Hampson, "Injured Police Officer Finds Power in Forgiveness," *Provo [Utah] Daily Herald*, March 5, 1995, p. D6.)

Whenever any of us feels offended by others, it is well to turn to Mormon's profound counsel to his son Moroni about how we should deal with those who offend us, and how we can acquire charity, the pure love of Christ: "Wherefore, my beloved brethren, pray unto the Father, with all the energy of heart, that ye may be filled with this love . . . that when he shall appear we shall be like him, for we shall see him as he is; that we may have this hope; that we may be purified even as he is pure. Amen." (Moroni 7:48.)

A heart filled with love has little room for anything else. Through forgiving those who caused them injury Marty Doumas and Steven McDonald had become immune to "the compulsive musings of the day and the seething dreams of night" described by Erikson (quoted previously in this chapter). For them, the instant had become an event and then a physical condition which they could not change. But they did have the power to change their mental, emotional, and spiritual condition, and this they did. Moral agency is one of God's greatest gifts to us; and one of our greatest gifts to Him and to others is the gift of forgiveness, forgiving others as He has forgiven us.

Ingratitude

In the Doctrine and Covenants the Lord declares that "in nothing doth man offend God, or against none is his wrath kindled, save those who confess not his hand in all things, and obey not his commandments" (D&C 59:21). In essence, the Lord here revealed that disobedience is a form of ingratitude; conversely, obedience is a confirmation of our gratitude. The Savior taught us: "If ye love me, keep my commandments" (John 14:15), thus obedience is a manifestation of our love for Him and our Father.

But what is the connection between moral agency and gratitude? King Benjamin explained it well:

> I say, if ye should serve him with all your whole souls yet ye would be unprofitable servants.
>
> And behold, all that he requires of you is to keep his commandments; . . . if ye do keep his commandments he doth bless you and prosper you.
>
> And now, in the first place, he hath created you, and granted unto you your lives, for which ye are indebted unto him.
>
> And secondly, he doth require that ye should do as he hath commanded you; for which if ye do, he doth immediately bless you; and therefore he hath paid you. And ye are still indebted unto him, and are, and will be, forever and ever; therefore, of what have ye to boast? (Mosiah 2:21–24.)

Grateful people easily recognize the source of all their blessings, and instead of complaining of life's injustices they express their gratitude for God's mercy and generosity. Gratitude for their blessings induces them to use their God-given moral agency to make righteous decisions in serving others of our Father's children, and this in turn brings the servers happiness. Grateful people have a sense of enabling power over their lives. Because they are happy they are also hopeful and optimistic and filled with faith. Continued service to others makes them more like the Savior, and thus they are blessed with the power to perform even greater service. Their minds are quickened because the Holy Ghost becomes their constant companion; and their moral agency continues to expand their capacity to grow and to help others grow and develop.

On the other hand, ingratitude limits our agency because it limits our vision of the world in which we live. Ungrateful people live in a world of limited options and demand a lot from life, often more than life has to give. As my father would put it, "Some people would complain if you hung 'em with a brand new rope." Ungrateful people would alter the great plan of happiness to exclude an opposition in *all* things. Elder Neal A. Maxwell observed that "too many of us seem to expect that life will flow ever smoothly, featuring an unbroken chain of green lights with empty parking places just in front of our destinations!" ("Murmur Not," *Ensign*, November 1989, p. 82.)

A person whose life is characterized by ingratitude is, by definition, very self-centered, and when he thinks only of himself his latitude of choice is extremely limited. For him, life's constant injustices demand revenge, and the list of personal injustices is lengthened by injustices to others until the option of forgiveness drops off the radar scope. The ability to forgive others is truly one of our most precious personal freedoms, and when we lose that our agency is seriously curtailed. Certain nations in the world have very restrictive diplomatic policies dictated by the insatiable demand for revenge and quick retaliation in kind. They are in bondage to their own policies.

Ingratitude becomes a precursor to paranoia and the feeling that no one appreciates us. Ingratitude cankers marriage relationships, as when an ungrateful husband criticizes his wife who has gained a few pounds after the birth of several children. Ingratitude in a wife can cause her to overlook her husband's ability as a good provider as she concentrates on his insensitivity to certain domestic details.

I attended the Puyallup, Washington, stake conference just a few days after a devastating flood had displaced several families from their homes. Brother and Sister Clifford Wimmer, a wonderful couple in their mid-eighties, were among those who were left homeless. During the Saturday evening session of conference I alluded to the sequicentennial commemoration of the Saints leaving Nauvoo in February of 1846. After the meeting I expressed my condolences to the Wimmers in this time of trial in their lives. Brother Wimmer embraced me, and with tears rolling down his cheeks onto the back of my suit, he said: "As you were speaking of the Saints in Nauvoo I reflected upon the life of my grandfather, who left Nauvoo and crossed the plains. When I think of the terrible hardships he endured, how can I expect to receive the same celestial glory he has received without experiencing a few trials in my own life?"

Sunday morning Brother Wimmer gave the invocation at the general session of conference. Notwithstanding his own dire straits, his prayer was an enumeration of blessings for which he and the entire congregation were grateful. His gratitude made him superior to his circumstances. Rather than feeling victimized, he was in charge. Some things lay outside his control, but he was able to control feelings of despair through what President Monson calls "an attitude of gratitude."

Ungrateful children limit the joy of parents who sacrifice much in their behalf, and ungrateful parents can become overly critical of wonderful children who always seem to fall a little short of perfection.

Ungrateful people demand more of life's rewards and expect less of life's demands for patience in suffering. Little do they realize that the purification process occurs more rapidly when we are on our knees than when we are standing on a pedestal.

Grateful people are invariably gracious givers, and in so doing they claim the Lord's promise that "he that loseth his life for my sake shall find it" (Matthew 10:39). For grateful people even the smallest blessing is a bonus in their lives.

Shifting Responsibility

In explaining the great plan of happiness to his son Jacob, Lehi explained that, because of our God-given agency, which allows us to make mistakes, and because of the atonement of Christ, which redeems us, we "have become free forever, knowing good from evil; to act for [ourselves] and not to be acted upon, save it be by the punishment of the law at the great and last day, according to the commandments which God hath given" (2 Nephi 2:26). Inherent in the plan of salvation is the accountability of every man and woman for their own sins (see D&C 101:78). But one of Satan's methods that cause people to lose their way back to a heavenly home is propagating the notion of shifting to others the blame for one's actions.

Some will say, "I'm inactive in the Church because my father was the bishop and he was a hypocrite." Or, "I don't go to church because my mother was the Relief Society president and she used to spank me." Or, "I'm inactive because my family never went to Church meetings while I was growing up." Or, "I never go to church because my parents forced me to go when I was young." Or, "Of course, I smoke and drink, just like my older brother does." Or, "Yes, I had a baby out of wedlock, just like my sisters."

Steve Howe was a very athletically talented young man who had a promising career as a baseball pitcher. But when the excitement of the roar of the crowd subsided, he turned to drugs for continued thrills. His mother made an insightful statement to the press regarding the roots of her son's behavior:

> It's easy to place blame where there is no blame. We have five children and we have one cocaine addict. I would die for my kids. But I will not take the blame for his addiction, any more than his father should. You know what I think Steve's problem is? Everything he ever said he wanted to do, he's done. He's any ordinary kid who got everything he ever wished for. All his dreams came true. And it wasn't enough. ("Quotes," *Deseret News Magazine,* 2 March 1986, p. 3.)

The great plan of happiness provided that men and women "are instructed sufficiently that they know good from evil" (2 Nephi

2:5), and this requires that each of us "will be punished for [our] own sins" and not for the transgressions of others (see Articles of Faith 1:2). After Corianton had consorted with the harlot Isabel, it may be that he attempted to shift the responsibility for this sin to Isabel because she had successfully seduced so many others. Alma told him, "She did steal away the hearts of many; but this was no excuse for thee, my son. Thou shouldst have tended to the ministry wherewith thou wast entrusted." (Alma 39:4.)

That wily Lucifer tries to induce us to postpone the day of our repentance by causing us to believe "that's just the way I am." In Harper Lee's *To Kill a Mockingbird*, the residents of Macomb County, Alabama, are described as having streaks. Some families have a "mean streak," while others have a "lying streak," a "drink-ing streak," a "gambling streak," or a "funny streak." (*To Kill a Mockingbird* [New York: Warner Books, 1982], p. 29.)

Implicit in this notion of streaks is the belief that once one has been born with a certain kind of streak there is very little one can do to dramatically alter that streak. Extensions of this notion are excuses for certain behaviors on the grounds of one's ethnic back-ground. Members of certain ethnic groups are seen as good street fighters, others are viewed as very romantic and morally compro-mising, while others are seen as hotheads, and still others are seen as cold and aloof.

These kinds of ethnic stereotypes are grossly unfair to groups of people and are of even greater consequence to individuals who try to explain away accountability for their actions because of their racial, ethnic, or socioeconomic background. The following chap-ter will address the enslaving power of cultural traditions, which are often at odds with the principles of the gospel. None of us can progress on the pathway to perfection until we accept the personal accountability for our actions, regardless of our earthly background, for, as the Apostle Paul taught the Athenians, "we are the offspring of God" (Acts 17:29). Each of us has a royal heritage that tran-scends our temporary station on earth, and if we are born with a streak of any kind it is a celestial streak, for "every spirit of man was innocent in the beginning" (D&C 93:38).

One dimension of shifting responsibility involves blaming others for our sins of *commission*. Another dimension is shifting responsibility to others for our sins of *omission*; for example, excusing ourselves from rendering compassionate service to others because plenty of other people will help those in need. Mancur Olson Jr. builds the case that, as groups increase in size, what should be everybody's business all too often becomes nobody's business. (See *The Logic of Collective Action: Public Goods and the Theory of Groups* [Cambridge, Mass.: Harvard University Press, 1971]). We encounter this problem in the fable of the little red hen. It seems that the little red hen discovered some kernels of wheat and asked others in the barnyard to participate in the raising of wheat that could ultimately be made into bread. Each of them shifted to others the responsibility for planting, watering, harvesting, grinding, and baking the bread. When it came time to take the loaf out of the oven, however, the interest in her project increased considerably. This gives rise to what Olson has called the free-rider tendency: "Though all members of the groups have an interest in obtaining the collective benefit, they have no common interest in paying the costs of providing that collective good. Each would prefer that others pay the entire costs." (P. 21.)

In his classic treatise, "The Tragedy of the Commons," Garrett Hardin addresses the problem of shifting responsibility for caring for common resources such as clean water, pure air, proper sewage treatment, adequate garbage management, and police and fire protection. In seventeenth-century England and in eighteenth-century New England, it was a common practice for individuals who lived around the village green to allow their animals to graze on the village commons. In the beginning there may be only five herdsmen with livestock, each allowing two animals to graze in the commons, which obviously have enough luxuriant grass to support the ten animals. With the passage of time, however, one enterprising villager may add merely one additional animal. The cost to the commons of this one additional animal is borne by all the other townsfolk, but the positive gain to the individual owner is 100 percent; he gets *all* the profit from that additional animal. This, of course, induces other herdsmen to each add just one additional cow or sheep, until the commons become overcrowded, and overgrazing transforms the commons into a mud bowl. Ultimately, there are no benefits that accrue to anyone. And this is the tragedy of the commons: shifting onto everyone else individual responsibility for maintaining a common good. (See "The Tragedy of the Commons," *Science*, 1968, vol. 162, pp. 1243–48.)

President Spencer W. Kimball warned us of the diffusion of responsibility which all too frequently occurs in the rearing of children. He emphasized the importance of parents assuming the major burden of training their own children: "There seems to be a growing tendency to shift this responsibility from the home to outside influences such as the school and the Church, and of greater concern, to various child care agencies and institutions. Important as these outward influences may be, they never can adequately take the place of the influence of the mother and the father." He continued: "It is the responsibility of the parents to teach their children. All other agencies are secondary. If parents do not teach their children, they will be held responsible." (*Church News*, April 7, 1979, p. 4.)

Three decades ago President David O. McKay proclaimed, "Every member a missionary." My observations indicate that, while nearly all members of the Church pray for the success of the full-time missionaries, a relatively small number of members actually help with missionary work by providing teaching referrals to the missionaries.

Some individuals will ask: "Why should I pick apples on the stake welfare farm when I have never received Church welfare assistance myself?" King Benjamin answers: "When ye are in the service of your fellow beings ye are only in the service of your God" (Mosiah 2:17). Others may query: "With thousands of other donors to the United Way or to the hospital blood bank, why should I contribute?" The Savior gives us one very good reason: "Verily I say unto you, Inasmuch as ye have done it unto one of the least of these my brethren, ye have done it unto me" (Matthew 25:40).

In the cosmic scheme of things, this entire universe and the five billion inhabitants on this earth are presided over by a Father in Heaven who is aware of every sparrow that falls (see Matthew 10:29). Can a lessened awareness of the needs of our fellowmen be justified by the fact that we happen to be members of large groups and organizations and by the perception that our contribution makes little difference?

In a secular society it may seem expedient and rational to adhere to the logic of collective action and only be concerned about our own self-interests, but in a church consisting of a community of Saints the Lord has given us a much higher standard of accountability: "Of him unto whom much is given, much is required" (D&C 82:3).

It seems significant that, in answer to the question regarding what we should do to inherit eternal life, the Savior's response was not a complicated theological exegesis or list of commandments but a simple recounting of the parable of the Good Samaritan, concluding with the counsel, "Go, and do thou likewise" (Luke 10:37).

Because we "are instructed sufficiently that [we] know good from evil" (2 Nephi 2:5), we cannot shift personal responsibility for either our actions or our inactions, our sins of commission or of omission, our offenses to God and others, or our missed opportunities for service to others.

Living in the Past

Sometimes individuals unwittingly limit their moral agency in the present by living in the past. The expression "That's just the way I am" has been a barrier to putting off the natural man in the lives of many. Levin, one of the main characters in Tolstoy's novel *Anna Karenina*, struggled to overcome this barrier. While on a journey far from home, Levin resolved to make some major improvements in his life. But upon returning home and seeing the familiar details of his previous life, he began to doubt whether it was really possible for him to change.

> All these traces of his old life seemed to clutch him and say: "No, you're not going to get away from us; you're not going to be different. You're going to be the same as you always have been—with your doubts, your perpetual dissatisfaction with yourself and vain attempts to amend, your failures and everlasting expectation of a happiness you won't get and which isn't possible for you."
> This was what the things said, but another, inner voice was telling him not to submit to the past, telling him a man can make what he will of himself. (London: Penguin Books, 1978, p. 108.)

The dramatic change in the life of Alma the Younger is one of the greatest success stories of the Book of Mormon. He recounted that he "had murdered many of [God's] children, or rather led them away unto destruction." These and other actions caused him to be "racked, even with the pains of a damned soul" and to be "harrowed up by the memory of [his] many sins." Providentially, his mind recalled his father's teachings "concerning the coming of one Jesus Christ, a Son of God, to atone for the sins of the world. Now, as [his] mind caught hold upon this thought, [he] cried within [his] heart: O Jesus, thou Son of God, have mercy on me, who am in the gall of bitterness, and am encircled about by the everlasting chains of death." Then the miracle occurred. Alma continues: "When I thought of this, I could remember my pains no more; yea, I was harrowed up by the memory of my sins no more." (Alma 36:14–19.)

One of the most powerful doctrines of the Book of Mormon is that we can—indeed we must if we seek salvation—undergo a mighty change of heart (see Mosiah 5:2; Alma 5:14). Such a change involves pressing "forward with a . . . brightness of hope" (2 Nephi 31:20), not living in the past. As we protect our moral agency from addictions, resist the spiritually enervating power of debt and discouragement, and when we nurture humble, grateful, forgiving hearts, our lives can truly reflect the hope that is within us.

For, behold, you should not have feared man more than
God. Although men set at naught the counsels of God, and
despise his words. (D&C 3:7.) ❧

Chapter Three

Culture and the Curse
of Respectability

The list of "parked cars" along the highway to perfection can be endless, and the issues we have discussed thus far are only illustrations of various forces in our lives which can rob us of the very moral agency we valiantly defended in the War in Heaven, but which we sometimes so carelessly surrender in the war here on earth.

One of the most insidious incursions upon our moral agency is what ironically may be called the curse of respectability. Many are surprised to hear such a statement. After all, respectability involves paying the bills on time, keeping a spit shine on the old shoes, keeping the house freshly painted, and manicuring the lawn and flower beds. What can possibly be insidious about respectability?

After Jesus had been apprehended and eventually brought before Pontius Pilate to be judged, the Roman governor's wife warned him to have "nothing to do with that just man: for I have suffered many things this day in a dream because of him" (Matthew 27:19). But when the choice was to be made regarding which prisoner to set free, Pilate assented to the release of Barabbas and to the crucifixion of Christ. "When Pilate saw that he could prevail nothing, but that rather a tumult was made, he took water, and washed his hands before the multitude, saying, I am innocent of the blood of this just person: see ye to it" (Matthew 27:24).

When the people cried out that Christ should be crucified, Pilate mildly protested with the question: "Why, what evil hath he done?" (Mark 15:14.) Upon further interrogation, Pilate declared: "I find no fault in this man" (Luke 23:4; see also John 18:38). But the mob "cried out the more exceedingly, Crucify him."

"And so, Pilate, willing to content the people, released Barabbas unto them, and delivered Jesus, when he had scourged him, to be crucified" (Mark 15:13–15). "And Pilate gave sentence that it should be as they required. And . . . he delivered Jesus to their will." (Luke 23:24–25.) Pilate's capitulation to the chief priests of the Jews is a classic example of caving in to the curse of respectability, notwithstanding his wife's warning and his own personal discernment that Jesus was a just man without fault.

The washing of his hands after delivering the Savior to the mob is an example of what President Marion G. Romney describes as "serving the Lord in such a way as not to offend the devil" ("The Price of Peace," Brigham Young University Devotional, March 1, 1955). And when they crucified the Christ, "Pilate wrote a title and put it on the cross . . . : JESUS OF NAZARETH THE KING OF THE JEWS." But the chief priests objected and urged Pilate, "Write not, The King of the Jews; but that he said, I am King of the Jews. Pilate answered, What I have written I have written." (John 19:19–22.)

The great and spacious building in Lehi's dream embodies the quest for—and the curse of—respectability, as shown by its numerous occupants "in the attitude of mocking" and scornfully pointing their fingers at those who were partaking of the gospel fruit of the tree of life. Implicit in this dream was the notion that those in the building constituted some kind of majority who pejoratively deride the faithful Saints, the minority. Within many nations throughout the world the respectable thing to do is to belong to the predominant religion of that country, whatever that religion may be. But just try to join a faithful band of two dozen Saints who meet in a rented room atop the butcher's shop and see how soon one's respectability is called into question.

Joshua was acutely aware of this problem as he cautioned the children of Israel against worshipping "the gods of the Amorites, in whose land [they dwelt]" (Joshua 24:15). The quest for respectability all too often involves overwhelming group pressure to follow the majority. Notwithstanding these pressures, Joshua pronounced that immortal declaration: "Choose you this day whom ye will serve . . . but as for me and my house, we will serve the Lord" (Joshua 24:15).

At the time of Elijah there were many who felt inclined to listen to the four hundred and fifty prophets of the heathen god Baal and to follow another four hundred prophets of the groves. This caused Elijah to pose the decisive question: "How long halt ye between two opinions? if the Lord be God, follow him: but if Baal, then follow him. And the people answered him not a word." (1 Kings 18:21.) To many of them it was more respectable to lean on the side of the big numbers than to follow a single man who claimed to be the prophet of the living God.

During the Savior's earthly ministry the Pharisees relentlessly sought to discredit some of His miraculous healings because they were performed on the Sabbath, such as the woman with an infirmity of eighteen years (see Luke 13:11–14), or the man who had been blind since birth (see John 9:8–16), or the lame man healed at the pool of Bethesda (see John 5:1–9). Through Pharisaical eyes, it was not respectable to "take up [one's] bed, and walk" on the Sabbath (John 5:8–12). As prophesied by Isaiah, they had begun to "call evil good, and good evil" (Isaiah 5:20).

Under this shroud of Pharisaical respectability, one of their number, Nicodemus, stealthily "came to Jesus by night" acknowledging that these miracles could not have been performed by man "except God be with him" (John 3:1–2). Nicodemus sensed that the Savior was no ordinary man, but it was not, as yet, respectable to follow him in daylight.

Many of the chief rulers of the day, after listening to the Savior's teachings, "believed on him; but because of the Pharisees they did not confess him, lest they should be put out of the synagogue: for they loved the praise of men more than the praise of

God" (John 12:42–43). That latter statement is the epitome of the curse of respectability.

The Savior was well aware of the Pharisees' insatiable need for social approval and respectability, as illustrated in his parable of the pompous Pharisee and the contrite publican:

> Two men went up into the temple to pray; the one a Pharisee, and the other a publican.
>
> The Pharisee stood and prayed thus with himself, God, I thank thee, that I am not as other men are, extortioners, unjust, adulterers, or even as this publican.
>
> I fast twice in the week, I give tithes of all that I possess.
>
> And the publican, standing afar off, would not lift up so much as his eyes unto heaven, but smote upon his breast, saying, God be merciful to me a sinner.
>
> I tell you, this man went down to his house justified rather than the other: for every one that exalteth himself shall be abased; and he that humbleth himself shall be exalted. (Luke 18:10–14.)

The curse of respectability sometimes seductively lowers our vertical heavenward gaze in deference to our horizontal scanning of the social landscape. In the parable of the Pharisee and the publican the former was interested only in the honor of men, while the latter was only interested in gaining forgiveness of his sins. When members of the Church come to their bishop to unburden themselves of their sins, concern with respectability must give way to a broken heart and a contrite spirit.

Sometimes misguided parents, suffering from the curse of respectability, stand in their children's pathway to true repentance. Fearing what their ecclesiastical leaders might think of them as parents, they discourage their children from making a full disclosure of their sins, for to do so might place a mission call in jeopardy or cause an embarrassing postponement of a temple sealing. I recall a discussion several years ago with a young man who, having come home drunk, had awakened his irate father. "What did your father say?" I asked. This now-contrite young man responded: "He only asked if anyone saw me drunk." In this young man's mind his father had little concern for the son's behavior but was greatly concerned about what the neighbors thought.

Entrance into one of the Church colleges or its university has unfortunately become tainted by the curse of respectability in certain families. What will our friends think if our children are not accepted at BYU or Ricks College? Surely people will gain the impression our children are either dull or unworthy. In fact, few people will harbor either of those thoughts. The Church has a large and excellent institute program available to those attending many non-LDS institutions of higher learning, and if those students use their time and moral agency wisely they can reap most of the benefits that accrue to those attending Church-sponsored institutions. Children who have been fortified with faith in their homes during their formative years will generally survive the rigorous testing of college life, regardless of where they go to school. Attendance at a Church-sponsored institution may provide a relatively safe environment for a time, but eventually our children are going to have to face the outside world on its own terms.

In most countries within Western society it is respectable to be wealthy; indeed, wealth is a driving force in Western society, and the greater the wealth, the greater the respectability. Only in developing countries is poverty respectable, because the overwhelming masses of women and men live in what most of us would consider to be poverty. And where is missionary work prospering throughout the world? Precisely in those countries where "the fashion of this world passeth away" (1 Corinthians 7:31).

Although the Savior said it would be difficult for the wealthy to enter the kingdom of God, we are grateful for numerous men and women of wealth who are devout Latter-day Saints and who freely and generously give of their means and their time and talents in furthering the work of the Lord.

Becoming a Peculiar People

After having assumed the leadership of the Church, Peter wrote an epistle in which he admonished "the strangers scattered throughout Pontus, Galatia, Cappadocia, Asia, and Bithynia" to be "holy in all manner of conversation," to "love one another with a pure heart fervently," and to lay aside "all malice, and all guile, and hypocrisies, and envies, and all evil speakings." Peter then declared them to be "a chosen generation, a royal priesthood, an holy nation, a peculiar people." (1 Peter 1:1, 15, 22; 2:1, 9.)

In addition to preaching of Jesus of Nazareth and Him crucified, in his second epistle Peter admonished the Saints of his day to "be partakers of the divine nature" in order to escape the corruption of the world. This, of course, is part of the process of becoming peculiar. He then provided a recipe for righteousness: "Add to your faith virtue; and to virtue knowledge; and to knowledge temperance; and to temperance patience; and to patience godliness; and to godliness brotherly kindness; and to brotherly kindness charity" (2 Peter 1:4–7).

Most of these Christian attributes do not reach the headlines on the ten o'clock news and they receive precious little space in *Time* or *Newsweek*. The Apostle Paul explained the reason for this: "The natural man receiveth not the things of the Spirit of God: for they are foolishness unto him: neither can he know them, because they are spiritually discerned" (1 Corinthians 2:14).

The *natural* man is also the *typical* man found in every culture throughout the world. The typical man in Germany drinks 143 liters of beer each year and the typical man in France drinks 79 liters of wine annually (see *Encyclopedia Britannica 1994 Book of the Year*). In America a fourth of the adult population smoke cigarettes, and in 1988 there were 1,591,000 abortions performed (see *Statistical Abstracts of the United States:1994*). Is it any wonder that King Benjamin declared that "the natural man is an enemy to God"? (Mosiah 3:19.) And herein lies the great challenge of lasting conversion to Christianity: How much of a country's culture can a Christian convert keep?

It would seem that we wish to become a peculiar people, but peculiar on our own preferred dimensions of peculiarity. Such was the case with the rich young ruler who asked the Savior: "What good thing shall I do, that I may have eternal life?" The Savior recounted the Ten Commandments, to which the young man replied: "All these things have I kept from my youth up: what lack I yet? Jesus said unto him, If thou wilt be perfect, go and sell that thou hast, and give to the poor . . . and come and follow me. But when the young man heard that saying, he went away sorrowful: for he had great possessions." (Matthew 19:16–21.)

We so very much want to remain respectable in the sight of our neighbors, yet all too often the people housed in the great and spacious building in Lehi's dream live just across the street.

After Joshua threw down the spiritual gauntlet admonishing the children of Israel to make up their minds, they declared in unison, "We will serve the Lord" (Joshua 24:21).

As for the idol worshippers at the time of Elijah, after the attempts of the priests of Baal had failed to call down fire from heaven, Elijah called down fire from heaven. "Then the fire of the Lord fell, and consumed the burnt sacrifice, and the wood, and the stones, and the dust, and licked up the water that was in the trench. And when all the people saw it, they fell on their faces: and they said, The Lord, he is the God; the Lord, he is the God." (1 Kings 18:38–39.)

While I do not wish to take anything away from a people who had suddenly become believers, it is interesting to note how quickly it became respectable to follow the prophet of God in the wake of extremely impressive audiovisual aids of heavenly origin!

Nicodemus also eventually overcame his trepidation and his fear of not appearing to be respectable. He defended the Savior before the chief priests and Pharisees, saying: "Doth our law judge any man, before it hear him, and know what he doeth?" This was a very daring course of action on the part of Nicodemus, for it caused his colleagues to ask, "Art thou also of Galilee?" (John 7:51–52.) The courage of Nicodemus in the face of opposition was confirmed at the crucifixion site when he "brought a mixture of myrrh and aloes" to assist in the preparation of the crucified body of Jesus (John 19:39).

And what of the chief priests who believed on Christ, but who feared the sanctions of the Pharisees? We read that after the Savior's crucifixion, resurrection and ascension, "the word of God increased; and the number of the disciples multiplied in Jerusalem greatly; and a great company of the priests were obedient to the faith" (Acts 6:7). Sometimes overcoming the curse of respectability just takes a little time.

Cultural Traditions

A recurrent theme throughout the Book of Mormon is the con-
straining influence of the false "tradition of their fathers" passed
down from Laman and Lemuel through subsequent generations
(see Mosiah 10:11–12; Alma 37:9; 60:32; Helaman 5:51;15:4; 16:
18–20). Tradition can be a double-edged sword. When based upon
the perpetuation of righteous principles, tradition can become a
marvelous support system in helping us to employ our moral agency
wisely. For example, a family tradition of holding family prayer each
morning and evening, of reading the scriptures each day, of faithfully holding family home evening each week, of regularly attending Church meetings, and of generously serving neighbors in
need—all these bode well for the spiritual development of our children.

On the other hand, many traditions find their origins in the
foibles of mankind. Such is the tradition found in many societies in
which women are expected to be chaste while men are allowed to
be promiscuous. In modern revelation the Lord has taught us:
"Every spirit of man was innocent in the beginning. . . . And that
wicked one cometh and taketh away light and truth, through disobedience, from the children of men, and because of the tradition
of their fathers." (D&C 93:38–39.)

John W. Gardner, a former U.S. Secretary of Health,
Education, and Welfare, observed the crippling power of some traditions in certain societies:

> If we accept the common usage of words, nothing can be more
> readily disproved than the old saw, "You can't keep a good man
> down." Most human societies have been beautifully organized to keep
> good men down. Of course there are irrepressible spirits who burst all
> barriers; but on the whole, human societies have severely and suc-
> cessfully limited the realization of individual promise. They did not
> set out consciously to achieve that goal. It is just that full realization
> of individual promise is not possible on a wide scale in societies of
> hereditary privilege—and most human societies have had precisely
> that characteristic. They have been systems in which the individual's
> status was determined not by his gifts or capacities but by his mem-

bership in a family, a caste or a class. Such membership determined his rights, privileges, prestige, power and status in the society. His ability was hardly relevant. (*Excellence* [New York: Harper & Row, 1961], p. 3.)

On the positive side, cultural traditions often provide a useful behavioral map for the members of a given society to get along well with their fellow citizens. But if we are to become members of a celestial culture we must overcome the natural man reflected in earthly cultures. However, the desire to get along and fit in with others can rob us of our ability to think for ourselves. Missionaries encounter many people who nominally subscribe to the predominant religion of their country without examining their own feelings on the subject of religion. In many countries, the dominant religion is embraced more as a cultural tradition than a spiritual force.

Some individuals voluntarily surrender their ability to form opinions on religion, politics and other important issues, letting worldly fashions determine their views on every subject. Oblonsky, one of the characters in Tolstoy's *Anna Karenina*, is an example of such a person.

> Oblonsky subscribed to and read a liberal paper, not an extreme liberal paper, but one that expressed the views held by most people. And although he was not particularly interested in science, art, or politics, on all such subjects he adhered firmly to the views of the majority . . . and changed [his views] only when the majority changed theirs; or rather, he did not change them—they changed imperceptibly of their own accord.
>
> Oblonsky never chose his tendencies and opinions any more than he chose the style of his hat or frock-coat. He always wore those which happened to be in fashion. Moving in a certain circle where a desire for some form of mental activity was part of maturity, he was obliged to hold views in the same way as he was obliged to wear a hat. (P. 19.)

John the Revelator admonished the Saints of his day: "Love not the world, neither the things that are in the world. If any man love the world, the love of the Father is not in him." (1 John 2:15.) James, his colleague in the holy Apostleship, lent a second witness regarding our relationship with the world when he wrote: "Ye adulterers and adulteresses, know ye not that the friendship of the world is enmity with God? whosoever therefore will be a friend of the world is the enemy of God." (James 4:4.)

As we cling to the iron rod and partake of the gospel fruit of the tree of life, we become enemies of the world, and some begin to scoff at us from their perch in the great and spacious building seen in Father Lehi's dream (see 1 Nephi 8). We are then called a peculiar people because we do not drink martinis before banquets, we do not toast others with a glass of wine, nor do we finish our meals with a cup of cappuccino coffee.

The world is concerned with "safe sex" and abortions, while the Saints of God are concerned with chastity and the sealing of families in holy temples. Many of the cultural customs and traditions of the world will transport us heavenward about as fast as a parked car.

One of the Savior's most brief yet profound parables describes the gathering process of proselyting: "Again, the kingdom of heaven is like unto a net, that was cast into the sea, and gathered of every kind" (Matthew 13:47). And therein lies the great challenge of preserving Christian values and doctrinal purity in the midst of great ethnic diversity among converts.

I was invited to speak to a group of wholesome, bright and beautiful Latter-day Saint youth in a stake that included Cambodians, Hmongs, Laotians, and Vietnamese. The youth leaders requested that I specifically address the issue of dating and marriage, explaining that it was customary in some of those cultures for young women to marry as early as thirteen years of age. That is an exquisite example of a cultural custom that cuts across the grain in the restored Church of Jesus Christ.

The difficulty in laying aside old customs became a source of great dissension among the early members of the Church during the ministries of Peter, Paul, and James. Certain men of Judaea, who were obviously great adherents of the law of Moses, had come down to Antioch and had begun teaching the brethren that "except ye be circumcised after the manner of Moses, ye cannot be saved." Paul and his missionary companion, Barnabas, took issue with this alleged doctrine, and the dissension in the ranks became so great that they decided to go to Jerusalem and counsel with the senior Apostles on this matter.

When Peter spoke at the Jerusalem meeting he alluded to the favor God had shown to the Gentiles, who had no previous experience with the law of Moses, that they might be privileged to hear the gospel preached to them. He then declared: "And God, which knoweth the hearts, bare them witness, giving them the Holy Ghost, even as he did unto us; and put no difference between us and them, purifying their hearts by faith." At the end, James summarized the counsel to be taken back to Antioch: "Wherefore my sentence is, that we trouble not them, which from among the Gentiles are turned to God: but that we write unto them, that they abstain from pollutions of idols, and from fornication, and from things strangled, and from blood." (See Acts 15:1, 2, 8–9, 13, 19–20.)

President Harold B. Lee once observed that too often we become involved in the thick of thin things. Sometimes cultural customs obfuscate eternal principles, but the Lord himself admonished that we prepare a "feast of fat things," as opposed to the thin things of the kingdom (D&C 58:8; see also Isaiah 25:6). It may be well to note that this admonition to concentrate upon the fat things of the kingdom was given long before cholesterol had been discovered.

It was not only the Jewish converts who had a difficult time letting go of some of the tenets of the law of Moses, which had become so deeply embedded in their culture. So did some of the Nephites. Nephi, Jacob, Jarom, Abinadi, and Alma all taught the law of Moses to the Nephites, and Alma explained why: "This is the whole meaning of the law, every whit pointing to that great and last sacrifice; and that great and last sacrifice will be the Son of God, yea, infinite and eternal" (Alma 34:14). But when the Savior actually appeared to the Nephites and ministered unto them, some of them, like many inhabitants of ancient Jerusalem, were caught spiritually flat-footed, "looking beyond the mark" (Jacob 4:14).

Thus the Savior exhorted the Nephites: "Marvel not that I said unto you that old things had passed away, and that all things had become new. Behold, I say unto you that the law is fulfilled that was given unto Moses. Behold, I am he that gave the law, and I am he who covenanted with my people Israel; therefore, the law in me is fulfilled, for I have come to fulfil the law; therefore it hath an end." (3 Nephi 15:3–5.)

This is the process of conversion. Old things are done away that all things may become new. But the question persists: How much of a country's culture can a Christian convert keep?

Certain members, and even some full-time missionaries, are much like Simon Peter. Though he was the chief Apostle and had been a fisherman by vocation, he did not at first fully understand the Savior's parable wherein He likened the kingdom of heaven "unto a net, that was cast into the sea, and gathered of every kind" (Matthew 13:47).

Peter was soon to learn the symbolic significance of the gospel net through a very unusual experience. In the tenth chapter of Acts we learn of a Roman centurion named Cornelius, who was in charge of an Italian band of soldiers stationed at Caesarea on the coast of the Mediterranean Sea. Cornelius was a devout, generous, and prayerful man. One day an angel of God appeared to him and commanded him to send a few of his men some thirty miles down the coast to the city of Joppa. In that city they were to go to the house of a tanner named Simon and to ask for a man named Peter.

While one of Cornelius's devout soldiers was traveling to Joppa in the company of two of his household servants, Peter went up to the housetop to pray. At length he became very hungry, fell into a trance, and saw the heavens open and a large sheet descending to earth. Upon this great tablecloth were many different kinds of animals, wild beasts, reptiles, and birds. The Lord had revealed to Moses that the meat of certain animals was unclean and should therefore not be eaten, and Peter had always observed this strict health code (see Leviticus 11). Thus Peter was greatly shocked as he gazed at these unclean animals and heard a voice say: "Rise, Peter; kill, and eat." Recoiling at this repulsive command, he replied: "Not so, Lord; for I have never eaten any thing that is common or unclean." Again Peter heard the voice: "What God hath cleansed, that call not thou common." This was repeated a second and a third time, perhaps in keeping with the law of witnesses, so that Peter would remember this vision. Then the sheet bedecked with beasts was taken again into heaven.

As Peter was reflecting upon the possible meaning of this strange experience the Spirit informed him that three men waited for him in the house below. Meeting the emissaries of Cornelius, he introduced himself by saying: "Behold, I am he whom ye seek: what is the cause wherefore ye are come?" The servants told him of Cornelius's vision and the instruction to send for Peter.

After lodging together for the night, together with some of Peter's brethren they all set out for Caesarea the next morning. Cornelius had invited his kinsmen and friends to be at his home when Peter arrived. Peter told all those who had gathered there: "Ye know how that it is an unlawful thing for a man that is a Jew to keep company, or come unto one of another nation; but God hath shewed me that I should not call any man common or unclean" (Acts 10:28).

While speaking to them, Peter had one of those great AHA! experiences when all the lights come flashing on in one's mind. He proclaimed: "Of a truth I perceive that God is no respecter of persons: but in every nation he that feareth him, and worketh righteousness, is accepted with him" (Acts 10:34–35).

As Peter taught these Gentiles the gospel and bore solemn witness of the resurrection of Jesus of Nazareth, "the Holy Ghost fell on all them which heard the word." And the Jewish members of the Church who had accompanied Peter from Joppa "were astonished . . . that on the Gentiles also was poured out the gift of the Holy Ghost" (Acts 10:45). These wonderful friends and kinsmen of Cornelius were then baptized with him.

Although Peter had just taught his Jewish brethren, members of the Church, that "God is no respecter of persons," they still were astonished that the Holy Ghost would fall upon Gentiles as well as upon Jews. This astonishment is not unlike an experience I had a few years ago on the campus of Brigham Young University. It was during an election year when a colleague of mine said, "I was surprised to learn that Phil is a Democrat. Why, I just saw him in the temple last Wednesday!"

It is my humble view that, while the restored gospel requires conformity to the commandments, covenants, and ordinances, the gospel does not require uniformity in all areas of endeavor. Throughout the Mediterranean countries and many other parts of the world it is customary to eat a leisurely late evening meal in the society of close friends and extended family members and to drink a glass of wine or two and to propose a toast of health and well-being to all present. According to modern revelation the leisurely evening meal may stay, as long as one's home teaching and temple work have been done, but the wine has got to go. The Savior changed the water to wine at the wedding in Cana, but in the Doctrine and Covenants sections 27 and 89 He changed the wine back to water.

There are some who would argue that scriptural dietary restrictions actually violate our human agency, removing much of the pleasure of life. However, Rabbi Harold S. Kushner takes exception to such a viewpoint. Says Kushner:

> I'm a traditional Jew, and I observe the biblical dietary laws. There are certain foods I don't eat. I suspect most of you assume I go around all day saying to myself, "Boy, would I love to eat pork chops, but that mean old God won't let me." Not so. The fact of the matter is, I go around all day saying, "Isn't it incredible? There are five billion people on this planet, and God cares what I have for lunch. And God cares who I sleep with. And God cares how I earn and spend my money. And God cares what kind of language I use." ("The Human Soul's Quest for God," *Brigham Young Magazine*, February 1995, p. 26.)

Alcohol, tobacco, and caffeine have been incontrovertibly demonstrated to be harmful to one's health, but their usage has other insidious implications and these deal with the incursion upon our moral agency. One of the world's greatest inventors was Thomas Alva Edison, who acquired more than a thousand patents on his inventions during a creative period between 1868 and 1934. But the inventor of the incandescent light, the phonograph, and moving pictures was not creative enough to discover a way to overcome his addiction to tobacco. While looking in the mirror one day he observed, "Holding a heavy cigar constantly in my mouth has deformed my upper lip, it has a sort of Havana curl." His smoking was frequently the source of an upset stomach, which caused him to exclaim: "The root of tobacco plants must go clear through to hell. Satan's principal agent Dyspepsia must have charge of this branch of the vegetable kingdom." (As quoted in Robert Conot, *Thomas A. Edison: A Streak of Luck* [New York: Simon & Schuster, 1979], p. 226.)

Still another important reason for the Word of Wisdom is the fact that obedience to this commandment sets the Saints of God apart from the world and helps make of them a peculiar people. We are happy to note that as medical and scientific evidence continues to support the Word of Wisdom it is becoming more and more respectable *not* to smoke or to drink alcohol.

Latter-day Saints are quick to describe our love of families, the importance of children and of family history, and the promises of temple blessings and their eternal consequences for families. But there are many other cultures throughout the world which also place great emphasis upon extended kinship structures and family life. Notwithstanding fears of contagious disease harbored by those of us living in antiseptic societies, the Polish Christmas custom of everyone at the table eating soup together from one large common wassail bowl is a great indicator of kinship closeness.

The Italian family structure is very close-knit, with great respect shown for the opinions of one's parents. Oriental cultures are legendary for their reverence for the aged and for deceased ancestors. But notwithstanding the importance of patriotic allegiance to one's country and one's affinity for family members, the Savior enjoined an even loftier allegiance as He taught: "He that loveth father or mother more than me is not worthy of me: and he that loveth son or daughter more than me is not worthy of me" (Matthew 10:37). Jehovah posed the poignant question to Eli the priest: "Wherefore kick ye at my sacrifice and at mine offering, which I have commanded in my habitation; and honourest thy sons above me?" (1 Samuel 2:29.)

There comes a time when choices must be made, and sometimes following Christ involves forsaking one's family. The Prophet Joseph Smith taught, however: "If children embrace the Gospel, and their parents or guardians are unbelievers, teach them to stay at home and be obedient to their parents or guardians, if they require it; but if they consent to let them gather with the people of God, let them do so, and there shall be no wrong; and let all things be done carefully and righteously and God will extend to all such His guardian care" (*Teachings of the Prophet Joseph Smith*, sel. Joseph Fielding Smith [Salt Lake City: Deseret Book Co., 1976], p. 87).

The affinity for culturally based music is very strong, as

evidenced by the publication of hymnbooks in several different languages throughout the burgeoning worldwide Church. Priesthood leaders and the general membership in foreign lands wanted to include in their hymnbooks some of the hymns unique to their cultures. This might seem like an easy enough task until one begins to collect the contents for a hymnbook in, say, French.

An apocryphal account tells of a time during World War II when the Allies needed to reach consensus on a crucial decision. Winston Churchill became very upset with Charles DeGaulle for his continual dillydallying over a decision. It is reported that De Gaulle finally told Churchill, "In a country like France where we have six hundred different kinds of cheese, it's very difficult to reach a consensus."

So it was with the selection of hymns in French. Not only must the members in France, Belgium, and the French-speaking area of Switzerland agree on the final list, but the same hymnbook would serve the Saints in eastern Canada and also in French-speaking Polynesia and in certain African nations. The Spanish hymnbook must please the Saints in Spain as well as their Latin American cousins. The Saints in Portugal and Brazil must find a common ground in Portuguese. The Italian Saints insisted on including an operatic anthem by Verdi that had religious overtones, and they contended that if the English hymnbook could contain "America the Beautiful," the Italian hymnbook could certainly find room for a few patriotic anthems in Italian.

The Church Music Committee, under the direction of the Brethren, established the guidelines that each hymnbook in every language would share a common core of one hundred standard hymns, fifty additional hymns from a longer recommended list, and then each language group would be allowed to select an additional fifty hymns dear to their culture, so long as the content of each hymn was compatible with the restored gospel.

The selection of the hymns was the easier part. Next came the difficult task of translation. It is extremely difficult to translate poetry into a second language and to make the words rhyme and still maintain poetic eloquence. But in translating hymn lyrics the difficulty is compounded by the need to match the message with the meter and the melody. Thus, to accommodate these musical constraints the English hymn "I Need Thee Every Hour" becomes "I Need Thee All the Time" in German and "I Need Thee Every Minute" in Serbo-Croatian. And the Poles have translated the hymn as "Stay Always Near Me."

Translators translated each hymn from English to their native tongue and then other translators translated it back into English to see how the lyrics survived the round trip. Sometimes the previous religious background of a translator would confuse the true message of some of the hymns of the Restoration, and these were retranslated until the Spirit confirmed that the message was conveyed in purity, notwithstanding a translation that was more eloquent than literal. But when one is in the presence of the prophet in Spain or Portugal or Pocatello and the Saints sing "We Thank Thee, O God, for a Prophet," this hymn is edifying and electrifying, and one is less concerned with vocabulary than with a confirmation of the Spirit that this man is, indeed, a prophet of God.

The Apostle Paul taught that in the Church of Christ "there is neither Jew nor Greek . . . for ye are all one in Christ Jesus" (Galatians 3:28). But there is some cultural baggage of which Jews and Greeks and Germans and Italians and Iranians and Japanese and Americans must rid themselves before they can become "one in Christ."

The natural man does what most other people do. But King Benjamin has taught us how to overcome the natural man and to no longer be at enmity with God. We must yield "to the enticings of the Holy Spirit," and become "a saint through the atonement of Christ the Lord." In other words, we must repent of our sins and claim the blessings of the miracle of forgiveness. We must then become "as a child, submissive, meek, humble, patient, full of love, willing to submit to all things which the Lord seeth fit to inflict upon [us], even as a child doth submit to his father." (Mosiah 3:19.)

We live in an age of political correctness when one must be extremely cautious in speech so as not to offend either gender, or to step on the toes of any ethnic group or nationality. But if I read King Benjamin correctly, the northern Europeans are welcome to bring their industriousness, orderliness, and punctuality with them into the kingdom, but their brusqueness must give way to "gentleness . . . meekness, and . . . love unfeigned" (D&C 121:41). The peoples of the Mediterranean and Latin America are enjoined to bring their warmth and their love of family and friends with them into the Kingdom, but intrigue and lust must be left behind. Americans must leave behind their materialism, their pride, and their cut-throat competitiveness and become as little children if they are to enter the kingdom of God.

In short, the conversion to true Christianity involves a two-fold process: First, an acceptance of the doctrines and ordinances of the Church as taught and administered by those who are duly empowered and authorized. Second, making the social transition from the natural man or woman to a man or woman of Christ, and part of a community of Saints who may be seen by others as a peculiar people.

In his great intercessory prayer the Savior prayed to His Father in Heaven in behalf of His disciples, whom He would soon leave behind: "I pray not that thou shouldest take them out of the world, but that thou shouldest keep them from the evil" (John 17:15). There are too many scriptural injunctions that we are to become a light on the hill (Matthew 5:14), to be an example to others (Matthew 5:16), to share the gospel (D&C 88:81), and to help our neighbors in need (Luke 10:25–37), for any Christian to assume that the Lord will be pleased with those who completely withdraw from the world into a self-righteous communal cell.

We are to become a peculiar people in the world yet not be of the world. Elder Russell M. Nelson has made us aware that the Hebrew word *segullah* has been translated as "peculiar" in the King James version of the Old Testament. An alternative meaning to *segullah* is "valued property" or "treasure." In the New Testament, the Greek word *peripoiesis* has been translated into "peculiar," whereas in other settings this Greek word is translated into "possession" as in "those selected by God as His own people." ("Children of the Covenant," *Ensign*, May 1995, p. 34.)

One of Satan's greatest tools is divisiveness, first to point out differences and then to play upon our pride in order to have us subordinate or persecute those who are different. Receiving persecution because of peculiar traits is part of the price of becoming Christian (see Matthew 5:10–11).

At the close of His ministry among the Nephites the Savior

posed the poignant question: "What manner of men ought ye to be?" He then answered the question: "Verily I say unto you, even as I am." (3 Nephi 27:27.) The Savior of the world was not known best for His ethnic background, though He was referred to as the Son of David and as a Nazarene. Nor was He known best for His previous occupation as a carpenter. Though I suspect He never owned any sheep of His own, He *is* widely revered as the Good Shepherd. Though He is well known for what He *taught*, He is far better known for what He *did* in taking upon Him the sins of the world and overcoming the bonds of death. His entire life was spent blessing, lifting, edifying, strengthening, comforting, and inspiring, and during His great intercessory prayer in Gethsemane He prayed that His disciples would be one (John 17:11).

The greatest unifier within The Church of Jesus Christ of Latter-day Saints is the holy temple. Whether in Brazil, Tonga, or Sweden, all temple patrons dress alike. The instruction is identical in every language as every patron is permitted to hear the gospel taught in his own tongue. The sacred ordinances are performed in exactly the same way in each and every one of the operating temples throughout the world. Within the house of the Lord there are no "manner of -ites" among us, for all are one with Christ (see 4 Nephi 17).

Temple covenants induce a common commitment to consecration and conformity in striving for the eternal things that matter most. Upon leaving the temple, faithful Saints throughout the world return home to highly diversified domiciles, different diets, and manifold modes of dress. So how much of a country's culture can a Christian convert keep? "If there is anything virtuous, lovely, or of good report or praiseworthy, we seek after [and keep] these things" (Articles of Faith 1:13).

I will be on your right hand and on your left, and my Spirit shall be in your hearts, and mine angels round about you, to bear you up (D&C 84:88). ✍

Chapter Four

War in Heaven and on Earth: But We Are Not Alone

Whenever wars and rumors of wars are the subject of articles in news magazines it has been a common practice to compare the two opposing forces in terms of the artillery at their disposal. Each side has so many tanks, so many missiles, so many nuclear warheads, so many submarines, bombs, and bombers, aircraft carriers, and so forth. In the previous chapters we discussed but a few of the myriad weapons in Satan's arsenal in extending the War in Heaven to a new battlefield on earth.

Our beloved President Gordon B. Hinckley has spoken eloquently of this extension of the War in Heaven:

> The war goes on. It is waged across the world over the issues of agency and compulsion. It is waged by an army of missionaries over the issues of truth and error. It is waged in our own lives, day in and day out, in our homes, in our work, in our school associations; it is waged over questions of love and respect, of loyalty and fidelity, of obedience and integrity. We are all involved in it—men and boys,

each of us. We are winning, and the future never looked brighter. ("The War We Are Winning," *Ensign*, November 1986, p. 45.)

We now turn our attention to the Savior's side of the conflict and to those who would be His Christian soldiers.

Testimony

We learn in the book of Revelation that during the War in Heaven those who overcame Satan and his followers did so "by the blood of the Lamb, and by the word of their testimony" (see Revelation 12:7–11). Our testimony was an invaluable weapon in the War in Heaven, and it is an indispensable weapon here on earth.

A testimony that is continually being nurtured and is continually growing will help us at every crossroad when important decisions are made. Indeed, a strong testimony supplants the need to make certain decisions under fire, because we already know well in advance the course of action we will take in those circumstances.

A loving Father in Heaven has given us many valuable means and resources to guide us in the wise exercise of our agency. When we are vigilant and observant and obedient we can realize the Savior's promise to His disciples: "I will not leave you comfortless" (John 14:18).

The Savior's Example and Atonement

Many of us have had the experience of buying a bookcase or a bicycle that comes as a do-it-yourself assembly kit. Some are more gifted do-it-yourselfers than others, and they can read the twenty-seven instructional steps and then assemble the bookcase or bicycle in a matter of minutes. Whenever *I* try to assemble something, the bookcase has wheels and the bicycle has shelves. I personally do much better when I can first watch someone else assemble the bookcase or bike; then I can follow the instructions much better as I anticipate each subsequent step in the assembly process.

Our loving Heavenly Father knew there would be simple folks like me who would have the detailed instructional books but would still need an example to follow. Jesus Christ set the perfect example for us. His life exemplified the only one who followed the Father's script perfectly. Without boasting, He acknowledged that "the Father hath not left me alone; for I do always those things that please Him" (John 8:29). He has extended the invitation to each of us: "Learn of me, and listen to my words; walk in the meekness of my Spirit, and you shall have peace in me" (D&C 19:23).

The Gift of the Holy Ghost

Before the Savior departed from His disciples He assured them that He would pray to the Father that they would receive "another Comforter," who would abide with them forever (see John 14:16). He taught them further that "the Comforter, which is the Holy Ghost, whom the Father will send in my name, he shall teach you all things, and bring all things to your remembrance, whatsoever I have said unto you" (John 14:26).

The Comforter will guide and direct our paths (see D&C 31:11; 79:2), and when we garnish our thoughts with virtue and develop charity toward every soul on this earth, then the Holy Ghost will be our "constant companion" (see D&C 121:45–46).

The Lord revealed that "the power of my Spirit quickeneth all things" (D&C 33:16), and I am simple-minded enough to believe that "all things" means "*all* things." He will not usurp or override our moral agency, but when He is given an invitation His Spirit will augment and accelerate our agency. When the Spirit, the gift of the Holy Ghost, is given a chance to influence us, decisions become easier, and despair dissipates as solutions to our challenges become clearly evident.

Book of Mormon prophets make it very clear that the Holy Ghost is willing to exert a very powerful influence in our lives when we are responsive to His promptings. Nephi, Mormon, and Ether explained that the Spirit *strives* with us to guide our lives on righteous paths (see 2 Nephi 26:11; Mormon 5:16; Ether 2:15). Moroni proclaimed that the Spirit *persuades* us to do good (see Ether 4:11–12). And King Benjamin explained that the Holy Ghost *entices* us to be righteous (see Mosiah 3:19).

The promptings of the Spirit will not supplant our moral agency, but the Spirit *will* underscore preferable options in our behavior and clarify a certain course of action in our hearts and minds.

The Scriptures

Another indispensable resource that assists us in using our agency wisely is holy scripture. The Apostle Paul explained that "all scripture is given by inspiration of God, and is profitable for doctrine, for reproof, for correction, for instruction in righteousness" (2 Timothy 3:16). Nephi gave the additional prophetic promise that when we "feast upon the words of Christ . . . the words of Christ will tell [us] all things what [we] should do" (2 Nephi 32:3). In short, the scriptures can become our life script, our instruction manual in mortality, if you will. And of course, if the universal teachings in holy writ are to benefit us, we must follow Nephi's additional counsel to "liken all scriptures unto us, that it might be for our profit and learning" (1 Nephi 19:23).

In addition to the guidance and direction they provide, another great benefit comes to us from reading the scriptures. Father Lehi beheld a vision in which he was handed a book of scripture, and "as he read, he was filled with the Spirit of the Lord" (1 Nephi 1:12). The inspiration and spirituality we gain from the scriptures is often as important as the information we receive. President Spencer W. Kimball put it this way: "I find that when I get casual in my relationships with divinity and when it seems that no divine ear is listening and no divine voice is speaking, that I am far, far away. If I immerse myself in the scriptures the distance narrows and the spirituality returns. I find myself loving more intensely those whom I must love with all my heart and mind and strength, and loving them more, I find it easier to abide their counsel." (Edward L. Kimball, ed., *The Teachings of Spencer W. Kimball* [Salt Lake City: Bookcraft, 1982], p. 135.)

With regard to words of modern revelation, the Lord Himself declared: "It is my voice which speaketh them unto you; for they are given by my Spirit unto you, and by my power you can read them one to another. . . wherefore, you can testify that you have heard my voice, and know my words" (D&C 18:35–36).

The Power of Prayer

The Apostle James eloquently observed that "the effectual fervent prayer of a righteous man availeth much" (James 5:16). Alma the Elder would certainly be an ardent advocate of this statement by James, for when the angel appeared to Alma's wayward son he explained that "the Lord hath heard the prayers of his people, and also the prayers of his servant, Alma, who is thy father; for he has prayed with much faith concerning thee" (Mosiah 27:14). Alma's prayer for his errant son was answered by the Lord through a ministering angel, and we are sometimes asked if such a heavenly manifestation did not, in fact, overwhelm the agency of Alma the Younger.

Before accepting the belief that some audio-visual aids are so impressive that we *have* to believe their message, it is well to recall the fact that Laman and Lemuel also had seen an angel, but alas, the angelic visitation had little lasting impact on their lives (see 1 Nephi 3:29–30; 4:3; 17:45). Alma the Younger and the Apostle Paul dramatically changed their lives following heavenly manifestations, but Laman and Lemuel "were past feeling" (1 Nephi 17:45), and were largely unchanged after the appearance of an angel. Clearly, then, these heavenly manifestations did not override the moral agency of those who received them.

Over the years a number of young people have approached me about the efficacy of prayer in their lives. A young man prays about his relationship with a young woman and feels inclined to ask her to marry him, only to have his proposal rejected by the young woman in question. The fact of the matter is, the Lord will not override another person's freedom of choice in order to meet our personal prayerful preferences.

All prayers are, indeed, answered, and it is well to remember that sometimes the answer is not in the affirmative. When the Son of God prayed in the Garden of Gethsemane that the bitter cup might pass, an affirmative response to His prayer would have thwarted the entire plan of salvation. But the Only Begotten Son demonstrated His meekness and humility and obedience as He added, "Nevertheless not my will, but thine, be done" (Luke

22:42). The divine answer was no, but "there appeared an angel unto him from heaven, strengthening him" (Luke 22:43). This is certainly a prototype and a promise for each of us as we too are required to drink from bitter cups in our lives.

Whenever we pray we would do well to remember Jacob's admonition to "seek not to counsel the Lord, but to take counsel from his hand" (Jacob 4:10). In an area training meeting with stake presidents Elder M. Russell Ballard observed how often it is that in our prayers we order the God of the universe all over the heavens as if we were ordering groceries by telephone.

In the wake of decision-making paralysis, undue anxiety, or panic attacks, when we prayerfully fall to our knees we can lay claim to the Savior's promise: "I will not leave you comfortless" (John 14:18).

Fasting

Great blessings are promised to those who live the law of the fast. Through the prophet Isaiah, the Lord posed an important question, followed by several profound promises: "Is not this the fast that I have chosen? to loose the bands of wickedness, to undo the heavy burdens, and to let the oppressed go free, and that ye break every yoke?" (Isaiah 58:6.)

When we subordinate our physical needs and desires to the dictates of the Spirit, we tap into a spiritual strength beyond our own. If we are in bondage to addictions, bad habits, or unkind thoughts, an unhappy past, or a bleak future, we can break the bands of weakness or wickedness through fasting. If we are carrying heavy burdens of past sins we have committed or others have committed against us, through fasting and proper repentance our hearts will be filled with love and forgiveness, and we can get on with our lives after having broken "every yoke."

Elder Vaughn J Featherstone introduced me to the following addendum to a well-known nursery rhyme:

> Humpty Dumpty sat on the wall,
> Humpty Dumpty had a great fall.
> All the king's horses and

All the king's men
Couldn't put Humpty together again.

"But the king could, and the king can, and the king will if we will but come unto him." ("A Man After God's Own Heart" [Provo: Brigham Young University, 1996], p. 33.) All we need to do is accept the king's invitation: "Come unto me, all ye that labour and are heavy laden, and I will give you rest. Take my yoke upon you, and learn of me; for I am meek and lowly in heart: and ye shall find rest unto your souls." (Matthew 11:28–29.)

Covenants and Ordinances

In the gospel sense a covenant is a very sacred, solemn agreement between God and one or more persons; however, "the two parties to the agreement do not stand in the relation of independent and equal contractors. God in his good pleasure fixes the terms." (*LDS Bible Dictionary*, p. 651.)

There is a rather common misunderstanding of the Lord's promise: "I, the Lord, am bound when ye do what I say; but when ye do not what I say, ye have no promise" (D&C 82:10). A young missionary may "covenant" with the Lord to arise each day an hour earlier in order to "bind the Lord" to his goal of baptizing a certain number of people each month. A retired couple may "covenant" to go on a mission if the Lord will reclaim a wayward child. Elderly members may promise to attend the temple each day if the Lord will spare them of their physical frailties.

Covenants with the Lord include our willingness to obey *His* commandments, not *ours*, and our desire should be to follow the Savior's example: "Though he were a Son, yet learned he obedience by the things which he suffered" (Hebrews 5:8). The attitude of "not my will, but thine, be done" (Luke 22:42) should govern our prayers and priesthood blessings.

Ordinances are outward manifestations of inward covenants and commitments. The Lord revealed that through the ordinances of the priesthood the power of godliness is manifest to men in the flesh (see D&C 84:19–21). There are many ordinances that manifest the powers of godliness and invite the Spirit into our lives by providing comfort and direction. When we renew our baptismal covenants through partaking of the sacrament we are *not* promised a life free from hardship and pain and the unpleasant vicissitudes of life, but we *are* promised "that [we] may always have his Spirit to be with [us]" (D&C 20:77), and His Spirit will comfort us and lighten our burdens.

Other ordinances include the blessing of infants, fathers' or priesthood blessings, administration to the sick, consecration of oil, and dedications of homes and graves. But of even greater importance than those ordinances are five ordinances that are essential to salvation: baptism, confirmation, the ordination of adult males to the Melchizedek Priesthood, the temple endowment, and sealing. These ordinances remind us of and bind us to decisions resulting from the exercise of our moral agency. A loving Heavenly Father has provided several means—such as regularly partaking of the sacrament and frequently participating in vicarious temple ordinances—through which we can be reminded of our sacred covenants and can make needed midcourse corrections in our lives.

President Boyd K. Packer has taught us that "ordinances and covenants become our credential for admission into His presence. To worthily receive them is the quest of a lifetime; to keep them thereafter is the challenge of mortality." ("Covenants," *Ensign*, May 1987, p. 24.)

Living Prophets

Our Father in Heaven has provided us with living prophets, seers and revelators who receive divine revelation and who help us understand His mind and will. In speaking of His servants, the Savior declared: "And whatsoever they shall speak when moved upon by the Holy Ghost shall be scripture, shall be the will of the Lord, shall be the mind of the Lord, shall be the word of the Lord, shall be the voice of the Lord, and the power of God unto salvation" (D&C 68:4). Elsewhere He declared that "whether by mine own voice or by the voice of my servants, it is the same" (D&C 1:38).

We sustain the fifteen men serving today in the First Presidency

and in the Quorum of Twelve Apostles as prophets, seers and revelators. They are watchmen on the tower who point out the course
of action we should take and who see beyond the bend in the road
and beyond the horizon.

In January of 1975, on a dark, rainy night in Tasmania, a 7,300-
ton barge smashed into two piers of the Tasman Bridge, which con-
nects Hobart, Tasmania, with its eastern suburbs across the bay. Three
spans of the bridge collapsed. An Australian family by the name of
Ling were driving across the bridge when suddenly the bridge lights
went out. Just then a speeding car passed them and disappeared before
their very eyes. Murray Ling "slammed on his brakes and skidded to a
stop, one yard from the edge of a black void." (Stephen Johnson,
"Over the Edge!" *Reader's Digest*, November 1977, p. 128.)

Murray got his family out of the car and then began warning
oncoming traffic of the disaster ahead. As he frantically waved his
arms, to his horror, a car "swerved around him and plummeted into
the abyss" (ibid.). A second car barely stopped in time, but a third car
showed no sign of slowing down and crashed into the Lings' car at the
edge of the bridge.

Suddenly a loaded bus headed toward Murray, ignoring his wav-
ing arms. In desperation, risking his very life, he ran alongside the driver's window. "There's a span missing," he yelled (ibid. p. 129). The
bus swerved just in time and came to a halt against the railing. Dozens
of lives had been saved.

I am grateful for these Brethren whom we sustain as prophets,
seers, and revelators who forewarn us of bridges not to be crossed.
(Spencer J. Condie, "A Mighty Change of Heart," *Ensign*, November
1993, p. 17.)

Parents

Elder James E. Faust related the account of President Kimball
interviewing a bishop regarding the frequency with which family
prayer was held in his home. This good bishop indicated that,
although they tried to have family prayer twice each day, they were
generally successful in holding family prayer but once a day.
President Kimball answered, "In the past, having family prayer
once a day may have been all right. But in the future it will not be

enough if we are going to save our families." Elder Faust reflectively added:

> I wonder if having casual and infrequent family home evening will be enough in the future to fortify our children with sufficient moral strength. In the future, infrequent family scripture study may be inadequate to arm our children with the virtue necessary to withstand the moral decay of the environment in which they will live. Where in the world will the children learn chastity, integrity, honesty, and basic human decency if not at home? These values will, of course, be reinforced at church, but parental teaching is more constant. ("The Greatest Challenge in the World—Good Parenting," *Ensign,* November 1990, p. 33.)

The Lord's injunction to parents is very sobering and unmistakably clear: "Inasmuch as parents have children in Zion . . . that teach them not to understand the doctrine of repentance, faith in Christ the Son of the living God, and of baptism and the gift of the Holy Ghost by the laying on of the hands, when eight years old, the sin be upon the heads of the parents" (D&C 68:25).

Sometimes we assume that positive parental influence not only diminishes but becomes completely absent after children leave the nest, but such need not be the case. While serving as a mission president several years ago, I had a conversation with a fine young man who had become a truly outstanding missionary. He was a little older and more mature than the other missionaries when he arrived in the field, but he knew why he had been called to serve and he served very effectively.

During one of our interviews he told me of his relationship with his father and his family. His parents had been active and prominent in the Church, and their expectations of him were high. Upon graduating from high school he received an offer of full financial support to further his education at one of the most prestigious educational institutions in America. His parents lived on the West Coast and his studies took him far from home to the East Coast. Far from the influence of his home and the Latter-day Saint friends of his youth, this young man began to drift from the Church.

While in this state of spiritual ambivalence, one day he heard a knock on his dormitory room door. As he answered the door, to his great surprise there stood his father. "What are you doing here, Dad?" he asked. His father simply said, "I've come to move in with you."

"But you can't do that," his son protested, "there isn't room for you to sleep here." "I'll buy a foam rubber mattress and sleep on the floor," the father replied. Continuing, he said: "I'm going to stay with you until we get your testimony back."

For the next several weeks, this patient and loving father studied the Book of Mormon with his son every day. They prayed together, and as trust increased they began to talk about things that matter most.

As my young missionary friend recounted the details of his reconversion, his eyes filled with tears of gratitude that his father's efforts had been successful in restoring his faith and testimony.

Gaining a testimony takes time, and watching others change their lives often requires long-suffering on our part. One of the sweetest stake patriarchs I have ever encountered shared a family heart petal with me. I surveyed his calloused, work-worn hands and asked him if he was retired. This seventy-year-old brother replied, "I only work half days now, from seven a.m. to seven p.m."

This humble man and his lovely wife had reared a large family. He said: "Last November we invited all of our children to prepare to attend the temple with us the following June, when Mother and I would celebrate our fiftieth wedding anniversary." He explained further that two of his children did not have current recommends, and so they would need some time to get their lives in order. "Well," he said, "last June we went to the temple and all of our married children were there with us."

I was inspired by the wisdom of these gentle parents who had truly used the principles of persuasion and long-suffering to gently influence the lives of their children. If only a few days or weeks previously they had invited their children to attend the temple, they would not have achieved one hundred percent participation. But these wise parents anticipated the future requirements of their children and provided adequate time for them all to qualify for the blessing of being in the temple together as a family.

Patriarchal Blessings

President Ezra Taft Benson encouraged every youth to receive a patriarchal blessing and admonished, "Study it carefully and regard it as personal scripture to you—for that is what it is. A patriarchal blessing is the inspired and prophetic statement of your life's mission together with blessings, cautions, and admonitions as the patriarch may be prompted to give." ("To the 'Youth of the Noble Birthright,'" *Ensign*, May 1986, p. 43.)

President James E. Faust has taught us that "a patriarchal blessing from an ordained patriarch can give us a star to follow, which is a personal revelation from God to each individual. If we follow this star, we are less likely to stumble and be misled. Our patriarchal blessing will be an anchor to our souls, and if we are worthy, neither death nor the devil can deprive us of the blessings pronounced. They are blessings we can enjoy now and forever." ("Priesthood Blessings," *Ensign*, November 1995, p. 63.)

Home Teachers

The Apostle Paul admonished the Hebrews to "be not forgetful to entertain strangers: for thereby some have entertained angels unawares" (Hebrews 13:2). Some of these angelic strangers have, no doubt, been home teachers who captured the true spirit of their callings to "watch over the church always" and who have had a profound and eternal impact upon the lives of those who have come under their influence. In the final chapter of the Book of Mormon, Moroni recounts the spiritual gifts with at least one of which each Latter-day Saint should have been blessed (Moroni 10:8–18; see also 1 Corinthians 12; D&C 46).

When I was ordained a teacher at the age of fourteen in our little rural ward, I was extremely fortunate to be assigned to be a home teaching companion to Valdean Alder. Valdean was about ten years my senior and had served a mission followed by a tour of duty as a soldier in the Korean War. He seemed to have wisdom and maturity far beyond his years.

Forty years ago all of the home teachers of the Church were

provided with a booklet containing twelve monthly home teaching lessons for the year. We would present the lesson for the month and then tear out a little coupon-like slip of paper which summarized the lesson we would leave with each family. The lesson for our first month together dealt with keeping the Word of Wisdom. The discussion went very well for the first three families (who probably did not need the lesson), but I was a bit apprehensive when we came to the Jensen home, because Brother Jensen smoked cigarettes. I was interested to see how Valdean would handle this situation.

Valdean began the discussion: "Tonight our lesson for the month is on not taking the Lord's name in vain." A very surprised expression registered on my face as Valdean winked at me and continued: "All of you Jensen kids can be very proud of your father. He's one of the few farmers in all of Franklin County who doesn't swear when a piece of machinery breaks down or when a cow kicks off the milking machine." As Valdean continued his commendation of their husband and father, Sister Jensen and each of the children seemed to sit a bit taller in their chairs.

Each month as we would return to the Jensen home, Valdean would continue to edify members of the family, especially building up the patriarch of the home in the eyes of his family.

About a year later my family moved to the big city, and we sort of lost track of the happenings of our little ward in the country. The years rolled by, and then one day we received a surprise phone call. It was one of the members of our former rural ward calling: "You'll never guess who the new bishop of our ward is—Brother Jensen." It was reported that there had been a great outpouring of love and support as he had been sustained. Each member of the ward had observed firsthand that callings in the Church are "for the perfecting of the saints," and much of that perfecting had been performed by a faithful home teacher who influenced the moral agency of others through gentleness, meekness, and love unfeigned.

Albert Knudsen has been a friend of mine for several years, and I assumed that he had always been an active, committed member of the Church. But it turned out that this was not so. Several decades ago Albert was very heavily involved in dairy farming and seemed to have little time left over for participation in the Church. It took a lot of time to milk all those cows, irrigate the pasture and alfalfa fields, harvest the hay, and feed the cattle. Somehow there just was not much time and energy left over for spiritual matters. With regard to his office in the priesthood, Albert described himself as "chronic Aaronic." For months and years Al's wife prayed that someone somewhere somehow would find a way to touch her husband's heart in this matter.

One late summer afternoon as the sun was beginning to set, Albert was standing in his field irrigating his crops. To his great surprise he saw the silhouette of a man coming toward him. It was particularly astonishing inasmuch as this man was wearing a white shirt and tie and some dress pants rolled up to the knees while he splashed his way through the muddy field. He was holding his shoes in his hands. As he approached, Al suddenly recognized that the man was Skippy Skipworth. Al said, "Skippy, what in the world are you doin' out here in the middle of this muddy field?"

With a grin on his face, Skippy replied: "Al, I've been assigned to be your new home teacher. I've been trying to locate you for several days, but each time I called your house your wife told me you were out in the barn milking, or out in the field irrigating. This afternoon I had a strong feeling come over me that told me I just had to see you today before the sun went down."

"Well, what do you want?" Al asked a little testily.

"I want to invite you to come to church this Sunday," Skippy replied forthrightly.

"Heck [modified translation]," Al replied, "if I come to church the roof will cave in."

Skippy persisted: "We'll just have to take that chance."

These two brethren discussed the wind and the weather and politics and athletics, and then Skippy prepared to leave: "Hope to see you in church on Sunday, Al." Then he splashed his way through the muddy water back to the road where he had parked his car.

Al later said, "I felt a very warm feeling come over me, and I began to think: 'If Skippy can come all the way out here to invite me to church, the least I can do is show up once.'"

So the next Sunday morning Al arose early enough to get the milking done in time to attend priesthood meeting. As the quorum meeting began, the quorum president asked Al if he would be willing to serve as the quorum secretary. Al replied: "You're just trying to give me a job so I'll keep coming back every week." "That's right," said the quorum president.

Al retorted, "Well, I'll do it for three weeks." And so he served for three weeks, and then three months, and then three years, and I became well acquainted with him when he served as a faithful ward clerk in the stake in which I served as the stake president.

Sister Condie and I were later called to serve in various assignments in Europe over a period of seven years, and during one of our visits home for general conference I tried to contact Al Knudsen to see how things were going. But I couldn't reach him. He and his wife were serving a mission in North Carolina. They have since returned, and now I frequently see Al when I attend the temple. He recently told me, "I'm not boasting, but I've read the Book of Mormon eighteen times during the past three years—my, what a marvelous book that is!" He is a shining example of a faithful home teacher's harvest.

Claim Your Blessings

Visiting teachers, home teachers, full-time and stake missionaries, and the membership of the Church at large are duty bound to help *all* of our Heavenly Father's children claim the blessings that he has in store for them. The following newspaper account metaphorically illustrates the fact that many of life's blessings will not automatically accrue to us. Most of them must be claimed.

Where's Your Luggage?: May Be for Sale

Associated Press, August 2, 1994—Scottsboro, Alabama—Ever wonder what happened to the book you left on that overnight flight from Los Angeles to New York? Missing some luggage that didn't make the connection to Chicago from Atlanta? It could be for sale in this north Alabama town. Books, bags and anything else that can get lost or left on commercial airline flights are up for grabs at the Unclaimed Baggage Center.

The store, which resembles an overgrown thrift shop, has contracts with major U.S. carriers like United, Delta and American to

purchase left-behind luggage and forgotten freight. It's not just suit-
cases that are for sale, though, so are the contents. And they're cheap.
Name-brand men's suits start around $50, and racks are full of $20
dresses. . . .

Whoever lost a green-and-purple NBC Sports garment bag with
a logo from the Wimbledon tennis tournament can buy it back for
$15. It's hanging on a back wall near a stack of crutches. Need some
handcuffs? Four bucks a pair. Over in the freight department, dozens
of made-in-Japan fuel pumps are $5 each. . . .

A loving Heavenly Father has provided each of His children
with countless blessings, but unfortunately, like lost luggage, many
of these blessings go unclaimed. In his keynote address as the
President of the Church, President Howard W. Hunter concluded
with the invitation: "Let us, as Latter-day Saints, claim those
'exceeding great and precious promises'" ("Exceeding Great and
Precious Promises," *Ensign,* November 1994, p. 9). May each of us
claim the blessings of living the law of tithing, the law of the fast,
the law of chastity, the blessings of keeping the Sabbath holy, of
pursuing family history and subsequent temple work, the joy of
sharing the gospel, the blessings of meaningful communication
with our Heavenly Father, and the blessings of all the covenants
and ordinances of the gospel.

A Decision-Making Strategy

Up to this point we have discussed the use of our moral agency
in facing decisions involving gospel principles and moral values,
but there are many other decisions in life that are not necessarily
right or wrong but that nevertheless involve the exercise of our
agency. For example, whether we go to an edifying concert or stay
home and read a wholesome book, or whether we have tuna fish
casserole or spaghetti for dinner are decisions of little or no eternal
consequence. However, there *are* decisions which seem at first to be
temporal in nature but which can have profound eternal consequences.

Elder Thomas S. Monson made the statement that the three
most important decisions we face in our lives are: "First, what will

be my faith? Second, whom shall I marry? Third, what will be my life's work?" ("Decisions Determine Destiny," *New Era*, November 1979, p. 5.) If, for a variety of reasons, less important decisions than these capture our time and attention early in life, as intimated by Elder Monson, our destiny can be greatly altered. Buying a house or a new car may seem to be a one hundred percent secular, non-religious decision, but if our decision impacts later upon our ability to pay a full and honest tithing, or requires us to work on Sunday and to miss the meetings we are commanded to attend, then our temporal decision can ultimately have eternal consequences.

Other decisions, like whether or not to pursue additional vocational training or a university education, changing career paths, choosing the people we date, and deciding on the location where we will live, all require the wise use of our moral agency, even though at first blush they may not seem to have immediate spiritual consequences.

Let us briefly analyze a general strategy many decision-makers use in making important choices. The first step is to *clearly identify the problem*. Using Elder Nelson's criteria discussed at the end of chapter one, it is well to identify each problem in the light of who we are, why we are here, and where we are going. I recall a young university student several years ago coming to my office to inform me he was dropping all of his courses at the university. When I asked him why he would do such a precipitous thing, he replied: "I just signed the loan on a new sports car, and I can't make the payments with only a part-time job. I'm going to work for a year or two, and when my car is paid for I'll come back to school." I lost track of him, but I had the sinking feeling that, like Esau of old, his priorities were not straight and he was selling his future for immediate pleasure.

When we see ourselves as children of God, here on earth to be tested, with a desire to return to a heavenly home, then most decisions will be made through the telescopic lens of the gospel. We can glean some insight from Moses and Brigham Young, both of whom were leaders with a vision of their final destination. They knew who they were, why they were here, and where they were expected to lead their people.

The selection of a certain career path may be viewed in terms of activities that are most satisfying, jobs that are more rewarding financially, and occupations that will adequately support a family and allow the parents to fully participate in the Church. If a host of career choices seem to be enjoyable, so much the better, but sometimes most of the fun in life occurs *after* we arrive home at the end of a hard day's work. I have a good friend who was reared in a family of ten children, and one day he confessed that he was twenty years old before he realized that the reason why his father worked fourteen-hour days as a farmer was to support the family, *not* because he loved his job so much. For him, his employment was an important element in the great plan of happiness because it assisted his family in fulfilling the measure of their creation in claiming all of the blessings of the gospel in their lives.

Happy is the man who can truthfully say: "I never went to work a day in my life—I have always enjoyed my job so much." More commonly we are likely to hear of fathers and mothers who love each other and their family so much that they do what it takes to support and sustain them. Occupational pursuits are seen as part of a greater plan, not as the means to immediate self-gratification. It would be well to initially define the problem in terms of its eternal consequences for the family. Isaiah asked the provocative question in this regard: "Wherefore do ye spend money for that which is not bread? and your labour for that which satisfieth not?" (Isaiah 55:2.)

A second step in maximizing the use of our moral agency in making viable choices is to *observe and collect preliminary information*. While attempting to translate on his own, Oliver Cowdery learned a great lesson from the Lord: "You must study it out in your mind; then you must ask me if it be right" (D&C 9:7). The implication was that the Lord will help us in achieving our goals once we have done our homework. This was the course of action followed by Moses as he dispatched Joshua and Caleb and ten others on a reconnaissance mission to gain preliminary information about the promised land during the second year of the Exodus. Others in their party dissimulated information about the obstacles they would face in conquering the land of Canaan, but Joshua and Caleb gave a truthful, positive report, and they maintained that vision of the promised land so that it sustained them until the time arrived when the children of Israel were permitted to enter Canaan. (See Numbers 13–14.)

There is an important distinction between being *indecisive* and being *undecided*. An indecisive individual has difficulty in making decisions when faced with alternative choices. On the other hand, a person who is undecided is holding a decision in abeyance while gaining enough data to make a wise decision. Although the Lord holds each of us personally accountable for the choices we make, it is always well to solicit as much information as we can about alternative decisions so that our final choice can be an *informed* decision. We can consult consumer magazines about the merits of an item we wish to purchase. We can confer with personnel counselors regarding potential future careers. We can consult with priesthood leaders, trusted friends, and family members regarding important decisions that may have eternal consequences. In the end, however, the choice is *ours*, and we must not relinquish to others our agency or our accountability as we prayerfully handle our agency with care.

A third important phase in the decision-making process is to *formulate possible alternative solutions*. The beauty of a rainbow is enhanced by its contrasting shades of color. So it is with making decisions. It is well to explore a number of options before deciding on which "color" we are going to pursue.

Thus the inventive genius of Thomas Edison lay not in scientifically based experimentation but in his persistent ability to pursue all possible avenues to the solution of a problem. While searching for the perfect filament for the incandescent lightbulb, the materials with which he experimented included "aluminum, boron, chromium, gold, iridium, platinum, ruthenium, silver, titanium and tungsten" (Robert Conot, *Thomas Edison: A Streak of Luck* [New York: Simon and Schuster, 1979], p. 138). Platinum showed great promise but its cost of ninety-eight dollars a lamp was prohibitive for household use (see p. 149). He tried a variety of non-metallic filaments such as "fish line, cotton, cardboard, tar, architects' drawing paper, celluloid, coconut hair, wood shavings, cork—even visiting cards!" (P. 157.) Undaunted, Edison experimented with a horseshoe-shaped piece of cardboard that had been carbonized through boiling in sugar and alcohol. This filament burned for sixteen hours. (See p. 161.) He experimented with still other materials as possible filaments: "southern moss, palmetto, monkey grass,

Mexican hemp, jute, bamboo, coconut palm, and manila fiber were dipped in rock-candy syrup and carbonized." He even tried spider-web. (Ibid., p. 173.) For him, no alternative was outside the realm of possibility. Each option was worthy of consideration.

In all of our personal experimentation with alternative solutions to decisions we face, it is imperative that we view each alternative in light of eternal values. A very large, talented young man who had had a distinguished university football career was a very desirable draft pick for many teams in the National Football League. He could have claimed a large salary, which would have provided him great security in life. But because many professional football games are played on Sunday, this young man decided to decline any draft offers. For him, playing on Sunday was not an alternative option. Every major decision in our life should be made in the light of acceptable alternatives and eternal consequences.

The brother of Jared had been given an extremely challenging task of building eight barges constructed "tight like unto a dish." To solve the problem of getting air into these barges he inquired of the Lord and was told to "make a hole in the top, and also in the bottom." The next challenge was how to provide light within the darkened barges. This time the Lord left the solution up to the brother of Jared: "What will ye that I should do that ye may have light in your vessels?" He asked. In response the brother of Jared extracted sixteen small stones from mount Shelem, brought them before the Lord, and asked Him to touch them with His finger "that they may shine forth in darkness." (See Ether 2–3.) This incident illustrates well the Lord's later revelation that "it is not meet that I should command in all things. . .[for] men should be anxiously engaged in a good cause, and do many things of their own free will, and bring to pass much righteousness" (D&C 58:27).

In this example, the brother of Jared's proposed solution was the right one, but there may be times in our lives when we must come to the Lord on several occasions to receive personal revelation in step-wise fashion, always trusting in the Lord's promise, "If any of you lack wisdom, let him ask of God" (James 1:5). It is significant to remember that before Joseph Smith went into the Sacred Grove to offer up his first vocal prayer, he had done his homework. That is to say, he had been searching and pondering the scriptures, and he had attended various revivals and had seriously considered the religious preferences of other members of his family. It was after he had identified the problem, collected preliminary information, and formulated alternative solutions that he went to Heavenly Father with the question of which church he should join.

It is also well to remember that Joseph received further revelation, priesthood power and keys over the course of several years. The answer to his questions continued to unfold throughout his mortal life. Sometimes we want *all* of our problems, past, present and future, solved by a single decision at a single moment in time. Much can be gained when we patiently follow the admonition, "Counsel with the Lord in all thy doings, and he will direct thee for good" (Alma 37:37).

A fourth step in making good choices may involve *predicting probable outcomes for each alternative solution.* This phase of the decision-making process involves assessing the risks of various strategies. Elder L. Tom Perry has drawn some significant lessons from the experience of Lehi's sons in procuring the brass plates from Laban, a risky venture indeed. After returning to Jerusalem, the inclination of these young men was to leave to chance the matter of obtaining the records, so "they cast lots, and the lot fell to Laman." But when Laman approached Laban about the brass plates he was accused of being a robber and was forced to flee for his life. Elder Perry concluded that "leaving the assignment to chance did not work."

The second alternative solution to the problem facing these young men was to return to their home and gather up the riches of this world and offer them to Laban as a bribe or payment for the brass plates (see 1 Nephi 3:22–25). But, as Elder Perry observed, when Laban thought of all his servants and then surveyed that youthful quartet with their gold and silver, "it was easy to determine that he could retain the plates and have the wealth also. . . . Things of the world did not produce the records."

Although his older brothers sought to dissuade him from continuing to pursue their original goal, Nephi relied on his faith in the Lord, and "making the decision to place his trust in the Lord produced the results." ("Making the Right Decisions," *Ensign,* November 1979, p. 35.)

There will always be some risks involved in the decisions we make, and thus we would do well to follow Nephi's example whereby "[he] was led by the Spirit, not knowing beforehand the things which [he] should do" (1 Nephi 4:6). Unfortunately, there are some people who have not yet drawn the distinction between faith and faith in the Lord Jesus Christ. There are some who have great faith (or wild-eyed dreams) of getting rich quick from a sure-fire investment scheme. Others have great faith that, notwithstanding extremely incompatible personalities, backgrounds, and values, somehow the marriage will just work out all right. But the scriptures and the teachings of the living prophets are clear. When they speak of faith, they speak of faith in the Lord Jesus Christ, and when we seek to "counsel with the Lord in all [our] doings" we counsel in wisdom, and our decisions will be grounded in faith in Christ rather than in unrealistic speculation.

For several years before the exodus from Nauvoo, the leaders of the Church had known that the time would eventually come when they would move to the distant west, to the Rocky Mountains. The big decision was when. They had carefully considered reports from explorers and others who were familiar with the climate and terrain of that western region, and they had maps which they had studied carefully. The decision of when to move west was made in light of the risks involved in trying to stay in Nauvoo.

While serving in an area presidency that included the Middle East, I was amazed at literally hundreds of Latter-day Saint families who live in distant countries so very far from their native home and close relatives. But I was impressed by their cohesiveness and the mutual support they give each other. In some countries one or two families may be the only presence of the Church in the entire country, and their examples to the citizens of that country and their righteous influence upon their work colleagues and neighbors have proven to be a great blessing. There are always risks involved in rearing a family in a predominantly non-Christian nation, but there are also risks in rearing families in so-called Christian countries which no longer espouse Christian values.

Predicting probable outcomes from our decisions involves a test of our patience and our faith, which testing is inherent in the great plan of happiness. A helpful step in making some difficult decisions is the use of the time-proven T-form in which we merely divide a piece of paper into two columns labeled respectively "Benefits and Advantages" and "Costs and Disadvantages."

Engaging in this little exercise will not make the decision for us, but this process will cause us to think about and evaluate the alternatives before we actually decide. Then, when we approach the Lord, we can qualify for His guidance, because we have followed His injunction to study it out in our own minds (see D&C 9:3–9).

Elder Bruce R. McConkie taught that "it is our obligation to go to work on our problems and then counsel with the Lord and get the ratifying seal of the Holy Spirit on the conclusions that we've reached; and that ratifying seal is the spirit of revelation" ("Agency or Inspiration," *New Era*, January 1975, p. 43).

Steven Kapp Perry captured the faith-stretching decision-making process in *Polly*, a one-woman musical depicting the life story of his great-great-grandmother Polly Matilda Merrill Colton (1816–1891). As a young woman from Shelby, Michigan, she made the most important decision of her life; she and her husband, Philander Colton, became members of the Church. Shortly thereafter they joined the other Saints in Nauvoo. Four babies were born to them who brought great joy into their lives, but a fifth infant son tragically died in infancy. Like other Saints they worked hard, built a house, and also helped to build the Nauvoo Temple, only to see all they had labored for left behind. They crossed the plains with the other Saints and, like many other husbands, Philander joined the Mormon Battalion. After arriving in the Salt Lake Valley they survived the invasion of the crickets and settled into a new home, only to be sent to settle the area of Ashley, present-day Vernal, Utah.

Once again great sorrow struck their family as one of their married daughters died suddenly, and Polly protested that children are not supposed to precede their parents in death. Toward the end of her life Polly sings about the choices she has made during her sojourn on earth and reflects upon the lessons she has learned from the decisions she has made and from the trials of her faith:

Make a Space for Joy

If I had known from the start
What would happen,
If I'd known in my heart,
Well then, . . . what then?

But I chose right.
I felt it all along.
If I had known what would happen
I might have chosen wrong.

Is that why You keep us guessing?
Is our ignorance protection?
Is it really just a blessing
In disguise?

Could you celebrate a birthday
Knowing life would soon be past you?
Could you spend the sweat to build a house
You knew would not outlast you?
Could you bear to love the children
Who would die before their season?
We'd miss so much of happiness
And maybe that's the reason
Not to know!

To free us from the burden of the future
And make a space for You!
To make a space for joy.
(Steven Kapp Perry, used by permission.)

Elder Nelson is right. When we remember who we are, why we
are here, and where we are going, we will tend to make correct
choices and muster the faith to patiently await their unfolding to
their conclusion. And a loving Father in Heaven has provided a
way to make midcourse corrections when some of our choices have
not been the right ones.

*And also trust no one to be your teacher nor your minister,
except he be a man of God, walking in his ways and keeping
his commandments (Mosiah 23:14).* ✻

Chapter Five

The Agency of Others:
Handle with Care

In the eighteenth chapter of Mosiah we read the account of Alma baptizing a number of people in the Waters of Mormon. He explains in very eloquent terms an important part of the baptismal covenant: "Ye are desirous to come into the fold of God, and to be called his people, and are willing to bear one another's burdens, that they may be light; yea, and are willing to mourn with those that mourn; yea, and comfort those that stand in need of comfort" (Mosiah 18:8–9).

Sources of Support

Within the organization of The Church of Jesus Christ of Latter-day Saints there are several institutionalized avenues whereby individuals can and should receive spiritual, social, and emotional support.

We often use the words *gospel* and *church* interchangeably. The gospel includes, among many other things, the commandments, doctrines, and ordinances necessary to return to the presence of our Heavenly Father. The Church is the organizational structure through which the gospel is preached and priesthood ordinances are authorized and performed. The Church is also a community of believers who worship together often (see D&C 20:55; Alma 6:6; Moroni 6:5), serve together, and mourn together—a kind of "support group," if you will.

In the earliest days of the restored Church, the Lord revealed section 20 of the Doctrine and Covenants, which has been referred to as the "constitution of the Church" (Harold B. Lee, in Conference Report, October 1970, p. 103). Among many other important matters, the Lord revealed the duties of the various offices of the priesthood and introduced home teaching to the Church, instructing priests and teachers to "visit the house of each member" and "to watch over the church always, and be with and strengthen them" (D&C 20:46–53).

Priesthood quorums, Relief Society, Sunday School, Young Women, Primary, the ward priesthood executive committee, the ward welfare committee, and the ward council all serve to meet the spiritual, social, emotional, and temporal needs of individual members and families.

Why Are Support Groups Needed?

With such a divinely inspired and comprehensive doctrinal and organizational infrastructure, one may well ask, Why do support groups seem to be necessary outside of the Church? The response to this query includes, but is not limited to, the following factors:

1. President Ezra Taft Benson referred to home teaching as "the priesthood way of watching over the saints" ("To the Home Teachers of the Church," *Ensign*, May 1987, p. 48). However, as long as the home teachers in many wards and stakes visit only half or three-fourths of the members, a large segment of Saints is not being watched over. And notwithstanding the Lord's admonition to match the strong with the weak (see D&C 84:106), sometimes those who need devoted home teachers the most are precisely those who receive the least care and attention.

2. Bishops and quorum leaders have a sincere desire to help

those fighting against tendencies toward alcoholism and drug addiction, or thoughts about homosexuality or child and spouse abuse. But some leaders are perceived by those in need to be limited in their counseling experience, and this can undermine the trust that should rightfully be placed in them as men possessing the mantle of their calling and the spirit of discernment. To some of those who are beleaguered by pathological problems, it seems that

> we only know how to respond to certain kinds of tragedies. It is as if there are acceptable and unacceptable problems.
>
> Lose your child to an automobile accident, and you'll have outpourings of sympathy. Lose him to drugs, and you'll get silent, judging stares.
>
> A father's heart fails, and neighbors will come to give emotional support. A father's business fails, and support is withdrawn.
>
> If a person has cancer, arms are thrown open with love. If he has a mental illness, backs are turned. (Music and the Spoken Word given by Spencer Kinard, "The Pain of Mental Illness," Tabernacle Choir broadcast of November 6, 1988.)

3. With the Church's highly mobile membership, sometimes troubled "members on the move" are not immediately integrated into new wards or branches, while secular support groups within the new community more readily accept new members. Some troubled members are in difficulty precisely because of their impatience and intolerance, and when ecclesiastical support is not promptly given they hurriedly seek a quick-fix in a secular support group.

The covenant to bear another's burdens and to comfort those in need of comfort may seem to be a scriptural endorsement for support groups, and indeed that is precisely what many support groups were organized to do. But sometimes a virtuous enterprise, carried to the extreme, can become more destructive than helpful. For the purposes of our discussion of support groups, I will arbitrarily divide them into three different types.

The first type includes *special interest groups*, whose members share interests in and concerns for specific issues, such as environmental groups or the Save the Panda Society. Members of Kiwanis, Rotary, and the Lion's Club also share a common interest in improving the quality of life within their community. Literary clubs or music appreciation societies or groups that foster the fine arts may also be included in this category.

A second type of support group consists of members with *common attributes*, such as parents of a Down's syndrome child or individuals suffering from a variety of chronic, degenerative diseases such as Parkinson's disease, multiple sclerosis, diabetes, lupus, or cancer. Participation in these groups can provide helpful information and support to participants who anxiously await the next developmental stage of their disease or who share hopeful news of recent research findings into possible cures for their particular medical problem.

A third type of support group includes those with a shared *pathological behavior* or those whose lives are influenced by the aberrant behavior of others. Such support groups would include child and spouse abusers; victims of abuse; those seeking to overcome thoughts and attitudes toward homosexuality, alcoholism, and substance abuse; and family members of those engaged in these and other behaviors.

Beware of Caveats

In his general conference address in October of 1990, Elder Boyd K. Packer included the following wise, cautionary counsel regarding affiliation with support groups: "There are support groups of many kinds which seek to fortify those struggling to withdraw from drug addiction or to master other temptations. On the other hand, there are organizations which do just the opposite. They justify immoral conduct and bind the chains of addiction or perversion ever tighter. Do not affiliate with such an organization. If you have already, withdraw from it." ("Covenants," *Ensign*, November 1990, p. 86.)

Closely akin to some support groups are so-called self-awareness groups. The Brethren issued the following caution regarding such groups:

> There is increasing concern regarding Church members' involvement in groups that purport to increase self-awareness, raise self-esteem, and enhance individual agency. Many of these groups advo-

cate concepts and use methods that can be harmful. Some falsely claim Church endorsement, actively recruit Church members, charge exorbitant fees, and encourage long-term commitments. Some intermingle worldly concepts with gospel principles in ways that can undermine spirituality and faith. Although participants may experience temporary emotional relief or exhilaration, old problems often return, leading to added disappointment and despair.

Church leaders and members should not become involved in self-awareness groups or any other groups that imitate sacred rites or ceremonies. Similarly, members should avoid groups that meet late into the night or encourage open confession or disclosure of personal information normally discussed only in confidential settings.

Church leaders are not to pay for, encourage participation in, or promote such groups or practices. Also, Church facilities are not to be used for these types of activities. Local leaders should counsel those desiring self-improvement to anchor themselves in gospel principles and to adopt wholesome practices that strengthen one's abilities to cope with challenges. Members are invited to consult with their bishops or stake presidents when seeking appropriate sources of counseling. (*Bulletin*, 1993, no. 2.)

Many of the caveats inherent in self-awareness groups are also to be avoided in other kinds of support groups. Much mischief can occur when an individual, in a moment of overwhelming trust, divulges intimate information to members of a group who have neither the loyalty nor the inclination to maintain this information in confidence. Thus some well-meaning support groups aimed at assisting in the rehabilitation of those who are battling with drug addiction or with thoughts of homosexuality have been perverted in their purpose by unwittingly becoming a social network through which one makes contacts with partners in future deviant behavior.

Our moral agency was so important that it became the focal issue over which the War in Heaven was fought. If we felt that moral agency was important enough to fight for before we came to earth, we must then jealously guard our agency and not thoughtlessly relinquish our freedom of choice to others.

A Pattern in All Things

In Section 52 of the Doctrine and Covenants, the Lord revealed: "I will give unto you a pattern in all things, that ye may not be deceived" (D&C 52:14; see also D&C 94:2). The Lord's pattern is expressed well by the Apostle Paul, who admonished the Corinthians in his first epistle: "Let a man examine *himself*" (1 Corinthians 11:28; emphasis added). In his second epistle he reiterated the need to "examine *yourselves*, whether ye be in the faith" (2 Corinthians 13:5; emphasis added). Please note that Paul's admonition was to examine *oneself*, not each other!

There are, of course, occasions, when one's life undergoes an examination in the presence of another person, such as confessing one's sins to a bishop. While certain support groups may have some bona fide and redeeming purposes, receiving confessions for sin is generally not one of them. The Lord's pattern in all things requires confessions to be held confidential between the confessor and the priesthood leader to whom the confessions are given.

There may be instances when priesthood leaders may refer a troubled member to LDS Social Services or to other reputable counselors and therapists. In the course of treatment, confidential information may be freely shared with a counselor or therapist if that is necessary to facilitate the process of healing. But a private confession is much different from a confession before a group.

Confession

One of the greatest burdens of all is the burden of sin, and the Lord has revealed that confession is an essential part of the process of repentance: "Behold, he who has repented of his sins, the same is forgiven, and I, the Lord, remember them no more. By this ye may know if a man repenteth of his sins—behold, *he will confess them and forsake them*." (D&C 58:42–43; emphasis added.)

With regard to confession, the question is often asked: To whom should confession be made? President Brigham Young admonished the Saints to keep your follies that do not concern others to yourselves, and keep your private wickedness as still as possible; hide it from the eyes of the public gaze as far as you can. I wish to say this upon this particular point in regard to people's confessing. We wish to see people honestly confess as they should and what they should.

If I have injured any person, I ought to confess to that person and make right what I did wrong.

. . . Tell to the public that which belongs to the public. If you have sinned against the people, confess to them. If you have sinned against a family or a neighborhood, go to them and confess. If you have sinned against your Ward, confess to your Ward. If you have sinned against one individual, take that person by yourselves and make your confession to him. And if you have sinned against your God, or against yourselves, confess to God, and keep the matter to yourselves, for I do not want to know anything about it. (*Discourses of Brigham Young*, sel. John A. Widtsoe [Salt Lake City: Deseret Book Co., 1941], p. 158.)

President Harold B. Lee recapitulated the essence of President Young's counsel when he taught us that "if your act is secret and has resulted in injury to no one but yourself, your confession should be in secret, that your Heavenly Father who hears in secret may reward you openly." President Lee added that "if you have 'offended many persons openly,' your acknowledgement is to be made openly and before those whom you have offended." (*Youth and the Church* [Salt Lake City: Deseret Book Co., 1970], p. 99.)

President Marion G. Romney explained further:

Where one's transgressions are of such a nature as would, unre-pented of, *put in jeopardy his right to membership* or fellowship in the Church of Jesus Christ, full and effective confession would, in my judgment, require confession by the repentant sinner to his bishop or other proper presiding Church officer. . . . One having forsaken his sins and, by proper confession, cleared his conduct with the Lord, with the people he has offended, and with the Church of Jesus Christ, where necessary, may with full confidence seek the Lord's forgiveness and go forth in newness of life, relying upon the merits of Christ. (In Conference Report, October 1955, p. 125; emphasis added.)

President Boyd K. Packer has instructed us that "when an offense is minor, so simple a thing as an apology will satisfy the law. Most mistakes can be settled between us and the Lord, and that should be done speedily. It requires a confession to Him, and whatever obvious repairs need to be made." ("The Brilliant Morning of Forgiveness," *Ensign*, November 1995, p. 19.)

One of the potential dangers of support groups is the creation of a climate in which personal weaknesses, fears, and anxieties are openly expressed. But what binds the members of support groups to maintain confidences after confessions of intimate information have been made public?

Some time ago I was assigned to meet with a distressed young mother of a large family, whose husband punched her in the face with considerable regularity, and she had written the Brethren in a cry for help. She indicated to me that she had called a crisis line for battered wives and had been referred to a support group comprised of women in similar circumstances. The goal and objective of this group was alleged to be the healing and recovery from the scars of repeated abuse leading to feelings of worthlessness or low self-esteem.

From this limited biopsy of one case, it seemed clear to me that this lovely, dear sister was not participating in a recovery group but rather a "wallowing group," whose members had individually and collectively become mired down by sharing their personal problems. She had received little sense of support, or of lifting, or of comfort, or of hope, or of an increased enabling power to cope. Indeed, during our conversation she often referred to those "poor other women" who constantly live in fear of their husbands. The collective problems of others were weighing her down, not lifting her burdens. As I listened to her describe her heart-rending experiences, I recalled President Harold B. Lee's observation that "you cannot lift another soul until you are standing on higher ground than he is" ("Stand Ye in Holy Places," *Ensign*, July 1973, p. 123). These women needed lifting, but I was not convinced that they were doing that for each other, and I felt that other sources of lifting and comfort might be more helpful.

In sharp contrast to the experience of this battered wife is the following brief vignette by a woman who had been abused as a child and subsequently had a very positive experience as an adult in a support group:

> Some people do not realize what a support group is and thus often mistake it for something spiritually dangerous or manipulative. Of course, appropriate care should be taken when choosing and working within a support group to avoid questionable practices or teachings. But from my experience, I have found my support groups to be very safe and non-threatening. They differ from so-called "self-awareness" workshops and weekend retreats because they are usually free of charge; they have been organized by and function with lay people; and they are not a "quick-fix" recovery program. Most groups consist of people who have a similar purpose of overcoming their pain and problems. They have come together to share their life stories confidentially and receive support from one another. Christ taught, "Bear ye one another's burdens" (Galatians 6:2), and such has been my experience in a support group.
>
> . . . I was so desperate that just getting through each day was a problem. If necessary, I was willing to start my own support group. As an answer to my prayers, I learned through a friend about a local support group of LDS women called "Come unto Christ."
>
> Participation in a support group allowed me to speak openly and honestly about the abuse I had endured. This was a powerful healing tool, because it helped break down the shame of secrecy and the resultant feelings of isolation.
>
> . . . I have learned through experience it is safer to share your pain and experience within the framework of a confidential support group or with a sympathetic person rather than sharing with someone who may not understand. It can be too painful for some people to hear, and that can produce difficult responses. (Anne L. Horton, B. Kent Harrison, and Barry L. Johnson, eds., *Confronting Abuse: An LDS Perspective on Understanding and Healing Emotional, Physical, Sexual, Psychological, and Spiritual Abuse* [Salt Lake City: Deseret Book Co., 1993], pp. 367–68.)

There is an old adage that "confession is good for the soul," and the confession of another person's sins to a support group may have some temporary psychological benefit as a catharsis, but unless and until the sick soul has been healed, confession in such a group setting may, at best, be like putting a Band-Aid on a cancer and, at worst, like reinfecting an old wound. Support groups can be very helpful in resolving certain problems, but they simply cannot become a substitute for the Lord's pattern in all things.

Too many people rely too heavily on others for solutions to their problems. The Lord promised an enslaved group of Nephites that He would "ease the burdens which are put upon your shoulders" (Mosiah 24:14). The sincere efforts of bishops, professional counselors, and even support groups can point people in the right direction, but the ultimate healing comes through the miracle of forgiveness, the reliance upon Christ's atonement in our lives.

Alcoholics Anonymous (AA) has enjoyed a solid reputation for many years as a very positive support group, and its goal is to change attitudes and behaviors for the better. I gained some valuable insight into AA from a reformed alcoholic I interviewed a few years ago concerning an ecclesiastical matter. He had not touched a drop of liquor for over two years, and now he had a radiant countenance reflecting a mighty change in heart. I asked him about the impact of Alcoholics Anonymous in helping him to change his life so dramatically. His response was profound: "Participation in AA group discussions was somewhat helpful, but the *healing* came one day in a drug rehabilitation center. The other members went off to participate in a group activity, and I found a place alone where I could kneel down and pour out my soul to the Lord. Something happened to me that day. I am a returned missionary, and I remembered all the things my parents taught me when I was young. I prayed for a long time, and when I arose from my knees, I felt I really could change and I could be forgiven."

According to his account, notwithstanding the comforting and encouraging influence of his support group the real, permanent healing occurred one-on-one with his Heavenly Father, *not* during group activities and discussions.

Godly Sorrow

There are times when individuals mourn because they have discovered the hard way that "wickedness never was happiness" (Alma 41:10). They have pursued the course described by Samuel, wherein they "have sought for happiness in doing iniquity, which thing is contrary to the nature of that righteousness which is in our great and Eternal Head" (Helaman 13:38). The Apostle Paul taught the Corinthians that "godly sorrow worketh repentance to salvation . . . but the sorrow of the world worketh death" (2 Corinthians 7:10). President Stephen L Richards added that "this godly sorrow is something more than admission after being discovered in sin" (In Conference Report, April 1954, p. 11).

Secular support groups consisting of caring friends and others suffering from common problems may temporarily assuage feelings of sorrow, but the godly sorrow to which the Apostle Paul referred requires a certain amount of time in a personal Gethsemane, alone on bended knee. No other mortal individual or group of individuals can lift the burden of godly sorrow; only the Savior who died for our sins is able to do that (see D&C 19:16–19).

Interviews

As with confessions, the Lord has also given us a pattern for conducting interviews. President N. Eldon Tanner provided the following counsel and guidelines to priesthood leaders:

> Careful, searching interviews need to be conducted always individually and privately. . . .
>
> Remember, the interview is based on consideration, on sympathy and love. This is so important. Let the people know we love them and are only trying to help them. . . .
>
> There are evil and degrading practices which, in the world, are not only condoned but encouraged. Sometimes married couples in their intimate expression of love to one another are drawn into practices that are unholy, unworthy, and unnatural. We receive letters from time to time asking for a definition of "unnatural" or "unworthy." Brethren, you know the answer to that. If in doubt at all, do not do it. . . .
>
> It is not in order for a priesthood leader to list in detail ugly, deviant, or bestial practices and then cross-examine a member of the Church as to whether or not such things are practiced. . . .
>
> Brethren, our interviews must be conducted in love, in modesty. Ofttimes things can be corrected if you ask: "Would there be a reason you may feel uncomfortable or perhaps even dishonest to the Lord if you were to sign your own temple recommend?". . .

If you approach the matter as outlined above, the member has the responsibility to interview himself. The bishop or stake president has the right to the power of discernment. He will know whether or not there is something amiss that ought to be settled before a recommend is issued. ("The Blessing of Church Interviews," *Ensign*, November 1978, pp. 41–43.)

Public "Interviews"

One of the potentially destructive dangers inherent in certain support groups is the inclination on the part of certain members to conduct the equivalent of "public interviews" with other group members and then to pass judgment in the spirit of confrontation. When an individual is hesitant to respond to a personal question, other group members may employ peer pressure to extract a response. "You don't trust us," they will say. Or, "We revealed *our* hang-ups, why can't you talk about *yours?*"

In a group setting, "interviews" of this kind are devoid of discernment, and they alienate the Spirit. Such "interviews" in a group setting constitute not only an invasion of privacy but also an infringement upon one's sacred moral agency. Though some may claim that healing begins when "everything's been unloaded," an accompanying anxiety arises afterward when the confessor realizes that very personal thoughts and information have been made public to group members whose confidentiality is far from secure. The classic social-psychological experiments by Asch, Milgram, and Sherif all confirm the great influence of group pressure in distorting personal judgments. (See Solomon E. Asch, "Studies of Independence and Conformity: A Minority of One Against a Unanimous Majority," *Psychological Monographs*, 1956, vol. 70, pp. 1–70; Stanley Milgram, "Behavioral Study of Obedience," *Journal of Abnormal and Social Psychology*, 1963, vol. 67, pp. 371–78; Muzafer Sherif, "A Study of Social Factors in Perception," *Archive Psychologia*, 1935, vol. 27, pp. 1–60.)

Priesthood leaders must be particularly sensitive to the esteem in which they are held in the eyes of those over whom they preside. One discouraging word from a bishop can disrupt the courtship of a couple who are bound for the temple. Too much encouragement to matrimony from a mission president during an interview at the conclusion of a young elder's mission may induce the young man to make a hasty marital decision that he may later regret. I have great personal confidence in the power of discernment vested in every priesthood leader who has the responsibility and the keys to counsel with the Saints, but as we counsel with others we must always handle their moral agency with great care. This does not mean we should not be firm and very specific in our counsel when the occasion merits it, but we should never usurp another person's accountability.

Criteria for Evaluating Support Groups

In evaluating the activities of support groups against the standard of the Lord's pattern for confessions and interviews, one might claim that such a comparison would be unjustified. After all, we are comparing secular support groups, devoid of a spiritual foundation, with divinely inspired procedures rooted in doctrine and implemented by proper priesthood authority. Notwithstanding the stark contrast in origins, the ecclesiastical model should be neither imitated nor supplanted by the secular group, for the Prophet Joseph Smith warned that "none but fools will trifle with the souls of men" (*Teachings of the Prophet Joseph Smith*, sel. Joseph Fielding Smith [Salt Lake City: Deseret Book Co., 1976], p. 137).

I have been intrigued with the diversity of support groups whose weekly meeting times are often published in various newspapers. These groups include parents of autistic children, parents of unwed mothers, children of divorced parents, and families with a member suffering from Alzheimer's disease. Certainly these meetings can be a source of solace for those with chronic degenerative illnesses and for those who face a life of long-suffering in silence. But what of other groups whose members are addicted to pathological behavior or are victims of aberrant behavior? How should the social, emotional, and spiritual support value of these support groups be evaluated?

I would humbly and respectfully propose the following criteria for determining the acceptability of these support groups and activities: Is the purpose of the group to bring attitudes and behaviors into conformity with the gospel of Jesus Christ and to follow the example of His life and teachings? Do group activities foster a greater desire to search the scriptures, to pray for guidance and comfort, to support local priesthood leaders, and to live worthy of personal revelation? If the answers to these questions are negative, in my judgment these support groups are to be avoided.

Let us take the problem of homosexuality as an example. This behavior is a great challenge for most bishops to deal with. Many ecclesiastical leaders have to struggle with personal compassion for the sinner while feeling abhorrence toward the sin. Certain support groups claim to have a very positive influence on those struggling with inclinations toward homosexuality who first gain a glimmer of hope and then a strong group assurance that *they really can change.* The support group may continue to be a source of strength and encouragement in sustaining the "mighty change of heart" (see Alma 5:13) undertaken by a repentant prodigal son or daughter.

On the other hand, the Lord described certain people in our day who "have strayed from mine ordinances, and have broken mine everlasting covenant; they seek not the Lord to establish his righteousness, but *every man walketh in his own way, and after the image of his own god,* whose image is in the likeness of the world" (D&C 1:15–16; emphasis added). When support groups or psychotherapists or counselors begin to walk "after the image of [their] own god," the greatest source of healing is automatically cut off. If a so-called support group has as its major focus calling "evil good, and good evil" (Isaiah 5:20), it should be shunned. If such groups merely try to buffer the suffering caused from social stigma while completely avoiding "godly sorrow [which] worketh repentance to salvation" (2 Corinthians 7:10), they should be avoided at all costs.

"Counselitis"

It has been my personal experience and observation that as one gets older one becomes more concerned with the "big picture" and less concerned with details. One begins to devote more attention to well-established great ideas and time-proven principles, and less attention to passing fads. Elder Boyd K. Packer provided some profound insight regarding what he calls "counselitis," an unduly heavy reliance upon others for solving our own personal problems. Said he:

> We must not set up a network of counseling services without at the same time emphasizing the principle of emotional self-reliance and individual independence. . . . If we are not careful, we can lose the power of individual revelation.
>
> Spiritual independence and self-reliance is a sustaining power in the Church. If we rob the members of that, how can they get revelation for themselves? How will they know there is a prophet of God? How can they get answers to prayers? How can they know for sure for themselves? . . .
>
> By probing too deeply, or talking endlessly about some problems, we can foolishly cause the very thing we are trying to prevent. ("Solving Emotional Problems in the Lord's Own Way," *Ensign*, May 1978, pp. 91–93.)

A wise bishop or stake president will provide individual members with a helpful strategy of exploring alternative solutions that will maximize their moral agency in solving their own problems. Many of these resources were discussed in the previous chapter. The counsel sounds so simple to those in distress, but if they will follow it the healing process can begin. Elder M. Russell Ballard has reported that he has never known a couple on the verge of divorce who knelt together in prayer each and every day. Fervent prayer really can "change the night to day." Preparing to attend the temple worthily and regularly is another simple suggestion that truly works for those who are meek and lowly of heart. Drinking deeply from the scriptures is yet another resource for resolving personal and family problems.

No matter how troubled a marriage relationship might be, priesthood leaders should generally never encourage a couple to divorce. There may be justifiable instances when an abusive spouse must be removed from a home in order to protect other family members, but generally the higher road is repentance, forgiveness, and reconciliation. If, after having counseled with their priesthood leaders, a couple then decides to part their ways, that is *their* decision. In contrast to this ecclesiastical counsel, I have received several reports of professional therapists who are anxious to control the agency of others in advocating divorce as an expedient solution to marital problems.

Wise priesthood leaders will generally not spend inordinate amounts of time with any given individual, but will give each member inspired counsel, encouragement, and perhaps a priesthood blessing, and then let that individual gain spiritual growth by improving the relationship with his or her Heavenly Father.

Professional therapists who meet weekly with their clients over a period of several months must be cautious of the problem of transference, where the client may become very emotionally, and perhaps even romantically, attached to the therapist. It is also not uncommon for a therapist to become emotionally involved with a client. These are dangers which can also affect priesthood leaders in their counseling relationships with members of the opposite gender if counseling sessions are too long and too frequent. Counseling an individual in distress has little value if an already complicated life becomes even more weighed down by the intrusion of a counselor's emotional involvement.

Hypnotherapy

For many years hypnosis has been used for therapeutic purposes by therapists who wish to help their clients lose weight, overcome alcoholism and tobacco smoking, or overcome various phobias, such as a fear of spiders, snakes, or large crowds. In more recent years there has been a wave of hypnotherapy used to help individuals overcome depression. In the course of hypnosis, certain therapists have claimed to discover the cause of depression, especially in female patients, to be sexual abuse in early childhood by a trusted brother, father, grandfather, uncle, or neighbor. Part of the prescribed therapy is to help patients retrieve their painful memories of abuse through the medium of hypnosis. After the "cause" of depression has been discovered, the patient is then told to sever all relationships and contact with the offending person.

This kind of therapy and counsel has had a devastating, disruptive impact upon many families, most of whom adamantly deny the allegations of sexual abuse within their family. Further investigation has led to what psychiatric professionals call "false memory syndrome." Under hypnosis individuals are very susceptible to the suggestions of the therapist, and some therapists plant ideas in the minds of susceptible subjects who then make accusations against their loved ones who supposedly abused them in their childhood, sometimes two or three decades previously. One very reputable psychiatrist and expert on hypnosis contends that

> there is a tendency for a therapist as well as lay observers to assume that these hypnotic memories are in fact historically accurate. This assumption is not justified. Typically, memories from different periods in the patient's life are combined; further, fantasies, beliefs, and fears may be mixed with actual recollections. . . .
>
> Because of these difficulties, the American Medical Association has taken an official position on December 5, 1984, which states that hypnosis does not result in increased reliable recall, that under some circumstances additional details may be remembered, some of which may be accurate and others inaccurate, and that recognition memory is not aided. For these reasons, the AMA has indicated that previously hypnotized witnesses should not give testimony in court concerning the matters about which they have been hypnotized. (Martin T. Orne, M.D., Ph.D., "The Validity of Memories Retrieved in Hypnosis," in B. Zilbergeld, ed., *Hypnosis Questions and Answers*, [New York: W. W. Norton and Co., 1986], pp. 45–46.)

Because many of those who have been accused of abuse are highly reputable and emotionally stable individuals, and because several patients have later recanted their earlier allegations, considerable doubt has been cast upon the reliability of information gained under hypnosis. National organizations have been formed, consisting mostly of parents who have been accused of sexual abuse by their children, with the intent of curbing further disruption of families.

One of the greatest tragedies of this form of so-called therapy has been the complete disruption of relationships between parents and children. Counsel to avoid all contact with other family members contradicts the professional advice of the Board of Trustees of the American Psychiatric Association, who admonished that "clinicians should not exert pressure on patients to believe in events that may not have occurred, or to prematurely disrupt important relationships or make other important decisions based on these speculations" ("APA Issues Statements on Memories of Sexual Abuse, Gun Control, Television Violence," *News Release*, [American Psychiatric Association, Washington, DC, December 22, 1993], Release No. 93–58, p. 2).

A few years ago the American Medical Association further warned that "memory enhancement," techniques (hypnosis being a primary method of retrieving memories of childhood sexual abuse) are "fraught with problems of potential misapplication" (Joan Stephenson, "AMA Wary of Using 'Memory Enhancement' to Elicit Accounts of Childhood Sexual Abuse," *Clinical Psychiatry News*, August 1993, p. 19).

Whenever a counselor or therapist forbids further contact between a parent and a child for the rest of their lives, this counsel runs completely counter to the heart of the gospel—the atonement of Jesus Christ. Of course there may be instances in which children of an abusive parent must be removed from the home to protect them from further harm. But the gospel advocates eventual forgiveness and reconciliation, *not* permanent alienation and disaffection.

The Healing Living Waters

When Jesus encountered the Samaritan woman at Jacob's well, the Savior said that if she knew who He was, she would have asked a drink of Him who would be able to give her living water which would be "a well of water springing up into everlasting life" (John 4:5–14).

In his vision of the Lord's second coming Zechariah foresaw that the Savior shall stand upon the Mount of Olives and "living waters shall go out from Jerusalem: half of them toward the former sea, and half of them toward the hinder sea" (Zechariah 14:8). Of this same event, Ezekiel prophesied that these living waters would "go down into the desert, and go into the sea: which being brought forth into the sea, the waters [of the Dead Sea] shall be healed. . . . And every thing shall live whither the river cometh." (Ezekiel 47:8–9.)

These dual prophecies are profound not only in their geographical and geological implications but also because of their metaphorical promise. Of all the places on earth, the Dead Sea is one of the most inhospitable to life. Even burning deserts of sand provide a home for hardy insects and reptiles and for certain plants with extremely deep roots. Concrete sidewalks and asphalt tennis courts sometimes crack, allowing a brave weed or two to survive above the surface. But the Dead Sea, because of its extreme salinity, harbors no life of any kind.

Thus, using the example of the Dead Sea, the Lord's prophets have chosen the worst possible case to illustrate the power of the living waters to heal that which is dead. The living waters of the gospel of Jesus Christ and His atonement can heal dead marriages, dead relationships between parents and children, dead friendships between business partners and neighbors, and spiritual death from years of alienation from the Church. His promise is sure: "Learn of me, and listen to my words; walk in the meekness of my Spirit, and you shall have peace in me" (D&C 19:23).

Trust No One to Be Your Teacher

Alma admonished the Saints of his day to "trust no one to be your teacher nor your minister, except he be a man of God, walking in his ways and keeping his commandments" (Alma 23:14). This counsel is vitally important with regard to therapists who would usurp one's agency through hypnosis.

In lieu of relying upon fully-accredited professional therapists and counselors, many members of Western society casually hand over their moral agency to newspaper columnists who freely give advice to the lovelorn, the disenfranchised and those who are downtrodden and discouraged. The advice columnist discerns the solution to other people's problems based upon a brief, impersonal, anonymous letter.

One of our nation's most reputable news magazines recently described the philosophy which underlies the syndicated advice column which Ann Landers has written for the past forty years:

> She is more of a pragmatist than a saint. Breaking the rules is bad

not just because it's wrong, she says, but because it is stupid—there is a penalty to pay. But when the rules change, she changes with them. In 1957, she challenged a reader to find "a single column in which I suggested divorce," but in 1972 she wrote: "I no longer believe that marriage means forever no matter how lousy it is—or 'for the sake of the children.'" And in 1981 she reported, "When I first got into this work, I thought a woman should remain a virgin until she married or died, whichever came first. . . . Well, I changed my mind about that." (Joannie M. Schrof, "Wake Up and Smell the Coffee," *U.S. News and World Report*, October 23, 1995.)

And who, might we respectfully ask, authorized Ann Landers to change divine laws and commandments? Ann Landers and her advice-giving colleagues are not alone to blame for shifting values. One seriously wonders about those who write for advice, seeking solutions to intimate problems of eternal significance as casually as ordering a hamburger at a fast-food restaurant.

Many radio and television talk shows are extensions of the newspaper advice columnists, and these shows have all of the inherent dangers of support groups with few of their advantages. Indeed, TV talk shows often become an extremely serious invasion of personal privacy as intimate details of one's life are broadcast to millions of voyeuristic viewers who should not be burdened with the problems of others when they are in no position to "comfort those in need of comfort." The publication and sensationalization of personal problems is not the Lord's pattern in all things. To discuss personal traumatic incidents in public will generally have little healing value.

The Lord's Pattern of Healing

In the general conference of April 1992, Elder Richard G. Scott eloquently described the Lord's pattern of healing from various forms of abuse. Among other excellent counsel he admonished those who had been abused to realize that "unless healed by the Lord, mental, physical, or sexual abuse can cause you serious, enduring consequences." He then counseled victims that when they prayerfully turn to our Heavenly Father and the Savior for help, the scars of abuse need not be permanent. He then exhorted victims not to "waste effort in revenge or retribution against your aggressor" but to leave the disposition of the offender to civil and church authorities. Victims of abuse were further instructed to seek the counsel of trusted priesthood leaders who may, where needed, recommend a qualified professional. (See "Healing the Tragic Scars of Abuse," Ensign, May 1992, pp. 31–33.)

You will recall Erikson's observation in chapter two that a certain traumatic event in life may be but for an instant, but the victim "relives it over and over again in the compulsive musings of the day and the seething dreams of night. The moment becomes a season; the event becomes a condition." The gospel of Jesus Christ has the power to reverse this process, that is to say, to change a condition to a passing event, and cause traumatic events to fade from memory. At the heart of the gospel is the atonement of Jesus Christ, the miracle of forgiveness, which involves forgetting as well as forgiving (see D&C 58:42–43; 64:8–10).

Sometimes the victim of abuse may be able to more easily forgive the perpetrator than can the victim's parents and other family members. One of the great examples of collective forgiveness is found in the Book of Mormon as the Nephites graciously accepted the Lamanite converts into their ranks. After Ammon and his companions had been instruments in the Lord's hands in converting a large number of Lamanites, these new converts wanted to be dissociated from other Lamanites who were not converted and remained vengeful, so they took upon themselves the name of Anti-Nephi-Lehi "and were no more called Lamanites" (Alma 23:17). Moreover they made a sacred vow to never again take up their weapons of war; indeed, they buried them deep in the earth (see Alma 24:15–16).

The Amalekites, compatriots of the Lamanites who resisted conversion, began to destroy the people of Anti-Nephi-Lehi, so Ammon suggested that these oppressed people go down to the land of Zarahemla and join themselves to the Nephites. The leader of the Anti-Nephi-Lehies resisted this, saying: "The Nephites will destroy us, because of the many murders and sins we have committed against them" (Alma 27:6). But Ammon rejoined: "Let us go down and rely upon the mercies of our brethren. . . . We will try the hearts of our brethren, whether they will that ye shall come into the land." (Alma 27:9, 15.)

And the hearts of their brethren were magnanimous indeed. Ammon went with Alma to see the chief judge, and after the judge had heard of the marvelous conversion of the Anti-Nephi-Lehies and of their oath to never more wage war, he sent forth a proclamation desiring "the voice of the people" on this matter. The vote was that "the people of Ammon" would be allowed to inhabit the land of Jershon. Moreover, declared the Nephites, "we will set our armies between the land Jershon and the land Nephi, that we may protect our brethren in the land Jershon. . . . And we will guard them from their enemies with our armies." (Alma 27:23–24.) The only requirement on the part of the Anti-Nephi-Lehies was that they supply provisions to assist in the maintenance of the Nephite armies.

The conversion of the war-mongering Lamanites who became the Anti-Nephi-Lehies was remarkable. But just as remarkable was the instant forgiveness of the Nephites, who apparently had friends and relatives who had been killed by the Anti-Nephi-Lehies prior to their conversion (see Alma 27:6). Conversion involves a mighty change of heart, a process experienced by both Anti-Nephi-Lehies and Nephites alike.

During World War II the German armies inflicted great suffering upon the inhabitants of the Netherlands. But shortly after the war had ended and reports reached the Dutch Saints that their brothers and sisters in Germany were starving, the Saints throughout the Netherlands gathered tons of potatoes and unselfishly shipped them to the Saints in Germany. This action, and others like it from many other countries, including America, had a cleansing, healing influence on both the recipients and the givers of the gift.

When the Savior came into the world He suffered "pains and afflictions and temptations of every kind; . . . that he may know according to the flesh how to succor his people according to their infirmities" (Alma 7:11–12). When we cast our burdens upon the Lord, traumatic events in our lives can be erased as love and forgiveness replace vengeance and pain. The moment of hurt fades and the event becomes but one wormy little apple on a long banquet table bedecked with a royal feast.

The Healing Power of Service

One of the great hidden keys to happiness and fulfillment in life is found in the Savior's paradoxical exhortation that "he that findeth his life shall lose it: and he that loseth his life for my sake shall find it" (Matthew 10:39). President Spencer W. Kimball confirmed the fact that rendering service to others is a major avenue to finding a mission and meaning to one's life:

> When we are engaged in the service of our fellowmen, not only do our deeds assist them, but we put our own problems in a fresher perspective. When we concern ourselves more with others, there is less time to be concerned with ourselves. In the midst of the miracle of serving, there is the promise of Jesus that by losing ourselves, we find ourselves (see Matthew 10:39) . . . .
> . . . The more we serve our fellowmen in appropriate ways, the more substance there is to our souls. . . . Indeed, it is easier to "find" ourselves because there is so much more of us to find! ("Small Acts of Service," Ensign, December 1974, p. 2.)

Service and sacrifice must be continual rather than occasional, constant rather than convenient. While it is the occasional heroic deed that grabs the newspaper headlines, it is the continuous day-in, day-out sacrifice for others that gives our lives a sense of purpose.

Concerned counselors can enhance their effectiveness through incorporating the scriptures into their counseling and into their personal lives, for the Lord has said, "the Book of Mormon and the holy scriptures are given of me for your instruction; and the power of my Spirit quickeneth all things" (D&C 33:16). I believe that "all things" refers to quickening the healing within troubled marriages, accelerating the miracle of forgiveness in the lives of the abused and their abusers, and breaking the shackles of the addictive behaviors of homosexuality, drug abuse, kleptomania, anorexia, and bulimia. We accelerate the healing process when we accept Moroni's benedictory invitation:

> Yea, come unto Christ, and be perfected in him, and deny yourselves of all ungodliness; and if ye shall deny yourselves of all ungodliness and love God with all your might, mind and strength, then is

his grace sufficient for you, that by his grace ye may be perfect in
Christ; and if by the grace of God ye are perfect in Christ, ye can in
nowise deny the power of God. (Moroni 10:32.)

The Prophet Isaiah prophesied that Christ would come and
that "He will swallow up death in victory; and the Lord God will
wipe away tears from off all faces" and "give unto them beauty for
ashes, the oil of joy for mourning." (Isaiah 25:8; 61:3.)

Well-meaning therapists can perform a helpful role in the healing process, but the ultimate healing occurs when we cast our burdens upon the Lord (see Psalm 55:22), and then He loosens the
bands of wickedness, lifts the heavy burdens, lets the oppressed go
free, and helps us to break every yoke (see Isaiah 58:6).

I say unto you, be one; and if ye are not one ye are not mine (D&C 38:27). ❧

Chapter Six

The Collective Convergence of Agency

After listening to a family home evening discussion on family history and pedigree charts, our then five-year-old son, Craig, set out to trace the genealogy of several stuffed animals that adorned his bedroom. He carefully explained to his four older sisters that his stuffed chicken was the mother of his stuffed turtle, who was the mother of his stuffed Snoopy dog. Having a bit of fun with him, they explained how that relationship was impossible inasmuch as turtles cannot be mothers to puppy dogs. His little brow was furrowed for a moment, and then the lights flashed on as he retorted: "You wanna bet? Mommy had me, and she's a girl and I'm a boy!" His young world was incongruent with his sisters' more sophisticated world, and this discrepancy often provided a rich source of humor in our home.

Inasmuch as this young man was reared in a household of older doting daughters, I frequently extricated him from his sisters' smothering mothering by engaging him in the masculine sport of wrestling. I systematically instructed him in various wrestling holds, including the full-Nelson. As I reached under his arms and interlocked my fingers behind his neck I exclaimed: "Now I have a full-Nelson on you!" His supple little body suddenly went limp and he easily slipped from my grasp. Voicing undisguised glee, Craig proclaimed: "That may be a full-Nelson, but it didn't fool me!" Once again, our two worlds of experience were unrelated.

Matrimonial Merging of Moral Agency

One of the greatest opportunities for joy and frustration in life is found within the confines of marriage and family life. There is a reason that men and women are referred to as the opposite sex—not similar, but opposite, for as Lehi taught Jacob, "it must needs be, that there is an opposition in *all* things" (2 Nephi 2:11; emphasis added). Even when a young woman marries the boy next door from the same neighborhood and similar family background, there are many challenges that must be resolved before the matrimonial merging of two "sets" of moral agency becomes smooth and flawless.

It was reported to me (tongue-in-cheek) that with all the sophisticated research relating to DNA genetic markers, one researcher had recently discovered a "doily gene" found only in the genetic makeup of women. Off the record, I feel confident that with a little more effort geneticists will soon discover the "dirty gym sock gene," which is confined to men. A column by Erma Bombeck possibly alluded to the presence of a "shopping gene" to be found only in women:

> A man shopping with his wife is like a dog line-dancing. He can do it, but he doesn't enjoy it.
>
> Spending $35 an hour is a woman thing. It's a contact sport like football. Women enjoy the scrimmage, the noisy crowds, the danger of being trampled to death and the ecstasy of the purchase.
>
> Men see it as a plastic frenzy.
>
> Did you ever see husbands in malls? They are lined up on benches like a bunch of pigeons on the courthouse roof. Their bodies are limp and their dead eyes stare into space. They are in a trance that will not be broken until the magic words are whispered in their ears: "You ready to go home?" ("Men in Malls Let Their Christmas Spirits Sag," *Provo [Utah] Daily Herald*, December 17, 1995, p. B6.)

The great plan of happiness provides countless opportunities for learning to resolve differences, to love, to tolerate and to forgive and, in the process, to become more like our Heavenly Father and His Son. Opposition in all things, including marriage, does not have to include dissension and continual conflict, but rather the peaceable resolution of differences. My good friend and counselor, the late Martin B. Hickman, once remarked: "I have only two objectives in life—to keep the commandments and to make Jo Anne happy."

The merging of agency into common choices actually begins with children in families and increases in intensity during the process of dating and courtship leading to marriage. This process is smoother when preferences in food, music and entertainment, literature, and religious activity are very similar. But gender differences will always be present throughout the entire marriage. I fear that too many men, although unwilling to admit it, share some of the views of Professor Henry Higgins expressed in My Fair Lady. In exasperation at Eliza Doolittle's independent feminine behavior, Higgins poses the musical question to his friend Colonel Pickering: "Why can't a woman be more like a man?"

Then he asks Pickering, "Why can't a woman be like us?"

In the final refrain Higgins arrives at his real hidden agenda as he poses the question: "Why can't a woman be like me?" (Alan Jay Lerner and Frederick Lowe, "A Hymn to Him," in My Fair Lady.)

Practice in resolving differences and reconciling preferences in exercising one's agency is provided in games children play. At a very early age children learn—sometimes the hard way—that they cannot always be the batter in the baseball game, even if the team is using their bat and ball. Compromise and sharing are also learned in relay races and sharing daily household chores. An excellent form of practice in learning the art of merging agency is playing in a band, or playing a duet, or singing in a group. There you learn in short order that it really does not matter how fast or slow you want to play or sing; you must reconcile your preference to the tempo the director or other musicians prefer.

The adjustments required by marriage can readily be likened to two musicians who are seated together upon a piano bench ready to play their first composition together. The young woman fancies a rather soft and gentle treatment of the music, perhaps played with mezzo-piano dynamics with an adante tempo. The young man envisions this composition as being played loud and fast. The fact of the matter is, women are not like men, and for that civilization can be eternally grateful. The refining, softening influence of women in the lives of children and families can scarcely be over-emphasized.

It is unfortunate that many young men are insensitive to the talents, the feminine characteristics, and the precious gift of moral agency their girlfriends possess. Any young man who, merely because he is physically stronger, violates a young woman's personal values automatically steps across the line and becomes an enlisted man among Satan's troops, who subscribe to coercion and compulsion. It is more than a matter of infringing upon personal standards or violating the law of chastity; it is a violation of the eternal principles defended in the War in Heaven. The use of physical strength to resolve differences is satanic in nature. After marriage, the marriage certificate does not give a young man license to pleasure on demand from his wife.

On the other hand, women must also learn the art of compromise and conciliation. Nor are women immune from violating the moral agency of men. Delilah's systematic seduction of Samson, robbing him of his physical and spiritual strength, is a classic case in point.

Notwithstanding the inherent differences between men and women, I have been disappointed with a number of couples who file for divorce contending that "we have *nothing* in common." As mentioned previously, there are, indeed, vast differences between men and women, regardless of any other background factors. However, once a couple have knelt across the sacred altar in a sealing room in the house of the Lord, they have the most important things of eternity in common, and this common bond can overcome all other differences. Several Church leaders have taught that the answer to marital difficulties is not divorce but repentance, involving humility and forgiveness on both sides. The Lord's method of resolving concerns is through persuasion, long-suffering, gentleness, meekness, and love unfeigned (see D&C 121:41).

Elisabeth

In 1992 the world premiere performance was held in Vienna for the Austrian musical "Elisabeth," by Michael Kunze and Sylvester Levay. This musical portrays the tragic life of young Elisabeth of Bavaria, the wife of Emperor Franz-Joseph of Austria. Elisabeth, or Sissy as she was affectionately called, married the young emperor in 1854 when she was only sixteen and he was almost twenty-four. Reared on the remote slopes of the Bavarian Alps, this teen-age empress found life in the royal court in the big city of Vienna to be very restrictive and even oppressive. Elisabeth found riding horses, hiking, gathering wildflowers, and traveling to faraway places much more exciting than attending receptions and chamber concerts at the royal palace. Her husband had a rather wooden personality and a dogged determination to do his duty, which he would pursue as emperor for sixty-eight years. His domineering mother was bound and determined to make of her new daughter-in-law a gracious and refined empress.

As the musical unfolds we see Elisabeth's freedom to choose a life of her own stifled on every side, and finally she expresses her frustrations to the young emperor in the song "I Just Belong to Me":

I Just Belong to Me

I don't want to comply, be cultured or constrained.
I don't want to be led, be loved or betrayed.
I'm not your possession; please set me free,
For I just belong to me. . . .

If you try to teach me you'll force me to flee
From the duty that binds me too tight.
If you try to change me then I'll tear away
And fly like a bird to the light. . . .

I'm searching for privacy and long for the morrow.
I'm waiting for friends to share joy and sorrow.
Don't demand my life too; *that* I can't give you,
For I belong to me,
Just me.

(Text by Michael Kunze and music by Sylvester Levay, "Ich gehör nur mir," from *Elisabeth*, Vienna, 1992. Translation into English by Heidi Condie.)

One could, of course, build a strong case that Elisabeth was extremely immature and should have grown up, honored her marriage vows, and accepted her regal responsibilities. But looking at the rabbit stew from the rabbit's point of view, we could also infer that when we feel an encroachment upon the sacred and eternal gift of agency, when our freedom to choose is being infringed, we inherently incline to resist the attempts of others to curb our freedom of choice. Not only did Elisabeth have to learn to adapt to the idiosyncracies of her husband, but she also had to accommodate the incessant, domineering intervention of a strong-willed mother-in-law who lived just down the hall in the royal palace.

The Lord's counsel is wise indeed: "Therefore shall a man leave his father and his mother, and shall cleave unto his wife; and they shall be one flesh" (Genesis 2:24; Moses 3:24; Abraham 5:18). President Spencer W. Kimball, speaking partly from his own experience, strongly urged newlywed couples to begin their married life in a domicile separate and apart from in-laws and parents:

> Couples do well to immediately find their own home, separate and apart from that of the in-laws on either side. The home may be very modest and unpretentious, but still it is an independent domicile. Your married life should become independent of her folks and his folks. You love them more than ever; you cherish their counsels; you appreciate their association; but you live your own lives, being governed by your decisions, by your own prayerful considerations after you have received the counsel from those who should give it. (Edward L. Kimball, ed., *The Teachings of Spencer W. Kimball*, [Salt Lake City: Bookcraft, 1982], p. 304.)

Newlyweds have a great enough challenge as it is without the additional interference of well-meaning parents and in-laws. While it is true that we marry entire extended families, not just a bride or groom, the newlyweds should be given every opportunity to adjust to married life without excessive outside intervention. Getting married is somewhat like emigrating to a new country, much like the experience of the Norwegian immigrant, who had recently arrived in the United States and was overheard to exclaim in exasperation: "I yust learnt how to say yam and then they changed it to yelly!"

The groom may have grown up on breakfasts consisting of hash browns, ham and eggs, while the bride's family had a slice of toast and a glass of orange juice. If he expects breakfast such as his mother prepared, he's in for a big disappointment, which is going to involve some future negotiations accompanied by compassionate compromise. Love, goodwill, tolerance, and perpetual, ready forgiveness are amazingly helpful lubricants in oiling the machinery of marriage.

The Symphony of Family Life

One of the lessons all parents learn early in their family life is that children are different from each other as soon as they arrive on earth. Shortly after the birth of our first daughter, my wife, Dorothea, and I attended a fireside given by a psychiatrist in our branch. He discussed the tremendous impact of the social environment on the development of children. Sister Johnson, a mother of ten children, interrupted him to point out that children come from the presence of their Heavenly Father with different personalities. Inasmuch as my wife and I were now experts as the parents of one, I mildly took issue with Sister Johnson in agreeing with the psychiatrist on the overwhelming importance of the home environment. Sister Johnson smiled sweetly and replied, "Wait until you've reared ten, then you'll know where I'm coming from."

One enterprising mother wanted to exert a positive influence on her young children while simultaneously helping them exercise their free will. To her six-year-old, she would say, "Suzy, would you like to make your bed before breakfast or after you've eaten breakfast?" It was clear to Suzy who was going to make the bed, but she had a little wiggle room regarding when she would choose to make it. The same held true for eight-year-old Sarah with regard to practicing the piano. The mother would ask: "Sarah, would you prefer to practice the piano before you go to school or when you come home from school?"

The four-year-old in this family had an intense dislike for vegetables, and so the mother would ask: "Billy, which are you going
to eat today, your peas or your carrots?" Little Billy soon caught on
to this form of alternative-option-child-rearing-practice, and one
day just about the time his mother wanted him to take a nap, he
said: "Mommy, I'm going outside to play, would you like me to go
out the front door or the back door?"

Each child arrives with different gifts and talents and with the
great God-given gift of moral agency. It is challenging for newlyweds to reach common goals, but the challenge increases as the
number of family members increases. The simple task of taking a
family photo is a good case in point. It may be a relatively simple
procedure to have a family photo taken when all the children are
below the age of twelve. The parents decide what everyone will
wear, so the little girls put on their Sunday dresses, the boys put on
a tie, slick down their hair, and it's off to the photographer.

But with the passage of years the children begin to exert their
agency. One of the older daughters will favor a formal portrait in
which all the girls wear pastel dresses and the boys all wear dark
suits, white shirts, and matching ties. One of the older sons might
argue for a rustic outdoor shot with everyone wearing blue jeans.
When a consensus is reached regarding the degree of formality, the
next hot issue is *when* the family photo will be taken. Conflicts
with school classes, work schedules, dates, and other social activities make a simple family photo involving seven or eight people a
remarkably complex achievement.

The Viennese social critic Karl Kraus contended that "most
books are prescriptions written by patients." I plead guilty in this
present humble endeavor. I am not very intelligent, and I admit to
being a slow learner, but, for what it's worth, I will share some valuable lessons I have only recently learned, mostly from our children.

First, members of a family can be likened to players in a small
chamber orchestra. Although there are compositions for flute solos
and piano duets, the most widely played pieces are those involving
several different instruments. The beauty of one violin is often
enhanced by the addition of a cello, a piano, and a viola.

Sometimes parents prefer the music of a cheerful flute and
aspire to rearing a family of ebullient flutists. In reality, the family

chamber orchestra can gain much in beauty and diversity if a violin, a French horn, a plaintive oboe, and a playful bassoon or trombone are added to the orchestra. The timpani, cymbals, drums, and other percussive instruments are usually played by preschoolers or teenagers, but no great composer ever ignored the valued contribution of the percussion section.

Another important insight gained by the conductor of the family symphony is that sometimes members change instruments. As life's lessons make their impact, the piccolo player may switch to the oboe, and the master of the kettledrum may prefer to play a harp. The important thing is not so much which instrument is played but that all are in tune and play in harmony with each other and with the principles of the gospel.

Often parents stifle the individuality and agency of their children through refusing to recognize the maturation process whereby the moral agency of children expands as their awareness of alternative choices increases. I am certainly not pushing permissive parenting, but sometimes parents unwittingly box their children into a perpetual state of dependence and immaturity. Elder LeGrand Richards related the story of the young lad who protested to his mother: "Mommy, I don't want you to call me Lamby Boy anymore. Call me Tiger!" Returned missionary sons may resist the premission moniker of "Kenny" or "Jimmy" and now prefer to be called Kenneth or Ken, James or Jim. Returned missionary daughters may now prefer to be called Lisa or Laura instead of "Daddy's Little Snookum." As long as maturing children are confined to past patterns, their agency may be somewhat restricted in being able to spread their wings and fly. Soaring to new heights always involves the risk of falling. Thanks be to the parents of Orville and Wilbur Wright for not discouraging their two sons from building a crazy invention called the airplane.

Many years ago I was assigned as a home teacher to a lovely widow and her son, who was in his mid-thirties. Each month my companion and I would subtly challenge young Fred to get him a wife. We would do it all in good humor, but he knew that the great plan of happiness required it of him. At the conclusion of our discussions his mother would say to us: "Brethren, thank you so much for encouraging Fred to get married. I tell him often that is what he should do." Then, after a brief pause she would wistfully continue: "But you know, Fred is so helpful to me. He mows the lawn, and shovels the snow, and he pays the utility bills and repairs the leaky faucets, and I just don't know what I would ever do if he actually did get married." Her subtlety in keeping Fred in bondage was much more adroit than our subtlety in challenging him to leave his mother and get married.

After conscientiously teaching our children the gospel in their homes, at some point parents must let go and let their children exercise their moral agency unfettered from parental intervention. One of the Brethren observed that some parents actually view children who leave home for faraway places as defectors from the family circle. It is gratifying to visit stakes of Zion throughout the world and meet wonderful members who left their places of birth to accept employment far from home and who, in the process, have rendered invaluable service in building up the frontiers of the Church wherever they live. These faithful Saints provide devoted, seasoned leadership and sterling examples to members of struggling wards and branches in isolated areas.

But wherever a family lives in the world there is always the risk of their children becoming worldly. Elder James E. Faust reminded us: "Parents have the obligation to teach, not force, and having prayerfully and conscientiously taught, parents cannot be answerable for all their children's conduct. Obedient children do bring honor to their parents, but it is unfair to judge faithful parents by the actions of children who will not listen and follow." ("The Works of God," *Ensign*, November 1984, pp. 59–60.)

An old Chinese proverb says, "Parents who spank children have run out of ideas." It used to be fashionable and expected that any disobedient child was taken to the woodshed for a little discipline. The instrument of choice was either dad's razor strap or a small branch broken from a shade tree on the way to the shed. After achieving early manhood, one of the Brethren once asked his mother why it was his parents had occasionally used the switch on him in his early youth but had abandoned the practice with the younger children. With a twinkle in her eye, his mother declared: "When we saw how you turned out, we realized it didn't do any good."

Physical punishment rarely does any more than teach a child how to be physically aggressive. Confining young disobedient children to their room may work well while they are young, and depriving them of the car keys may get their attention after age sixteen. But at some point in time parents have to be willing to rely on what the children have been taught and shown at home, and then allow them to make subsequent decisions on their own. I suspect that one source of tears at the airport as parents kiss their departing sons and daughters goodbye is the sinking feeling that certain mission presidents may be inheriting a less than perfectly finished product. Parents are hopeful the mission president will be a kindly and compassionate man who will allow those sons and daughters a little more time to mature.

I was troubled for some time by the Old Testament incident in which the boy Samuel was living with Eli, the elderly temple priest. One evening the Lord revealed to young Samuel that he would judge Eli's house "for the iniquity which he knoweth; because his sons made themselves vile, and he restrained them not" (1 Samuel 3:13). I wondered why this elderly man should be judged harshly when it was probably physically impossible for him to restrain his younger and physically stronger sons.

As with most scriptures, we gain great insight into the meaning of a given verse when we read the chapters preceding and following the verse in question so that we fully benefit from the entire context in which the verse appears. Returning to the previous chapter we learn that Eli's sons were very wicked and "knew not the Lord" (1 Samuel 2:12). Nevertheless, Eli permitted his sons to assist in the preparation of the sacred offerings for the temple, in which they exercised unrighteous dominion; "Wherefore the sin of the young men was very great before the Lord: for men abhorred the offering of the Lord" (1 Samuel 2:17).

Taken in context, it seems safe to infer that the Lord's wrath against Eli was founded not so much in the fact that he did not restrain his sons from sin, something which may have been difficult if not impossible for him to do, but rather he was judged because he did not restrain them from participating in the ordinances of the temple, something he *did* have power to do as the presiding priest. There is a lesson here for bishops and stake presidents.

One fast Sunday when our children were very young and very hungry following what seemed to them a very slow fast Sunday, they engaged in a little jousting about why they had to wait so long to eat and whose turn it was to set the table and who had to wash the dishes afterward, and the spirit of the Sabbath was quickly evaporating before our very eyes. Suddenly I slammed my open hand against the top of the table and got their attention and asked them to all sit down. As they did so, I read them King Benjamin's exhortation that parents "not suffer [their] children that they . . . transgress the laws of God, and fight and quarrel one with another" (Mosiah 4:14). I then said, "That's a commandment given to Mother and me, that we do not allow our children to quarrel one with another. Now, we would be very grateful if you would help us keep that commandment." I am pleased to report that this counsel dramatically changed their behavior—for about ten or fifteen minutes.

A wise father of a very large family pointed out to me that the venerable Proverb reads: "Train up a child in the way he should go: and *when he is old*, he will not depart from it" (Proverbs 22:6; emphasis added). The inference drawn by this sagacious friend was that even those who have been properly taught as children occasionally want to see the world, and in the process become worldly for a time. But my friend's assurance is that, like the prodigal son, if correctly taught in their youth, when children become older they will return to the path their parents trod. But the promised blessing, much like a patriarchal blessing, is contingent upon obedience—in this case the obedience of the parents in actually training up the child with family prayer, scripture reading, family home evening, father's blessings, and an abundance of love. Such a promise, devoid of observable results, can be a great test of the patience, faith, and long-suffering of parents.

Elder James E. Faust shared this compassionate observation regarding the challenge of parenting: "In my opinion, the teaching, rearing, and training of children requires more intelligence, intuitive understanding, humility, strength, wisdom, spirituality, perseverance, and hard work than any other challenge we might have in life. This is especially so when moral foundations of honor and decency are eroding around us." ("The Greatest Challenge in the World—Good Parenting," *Ensign*, November 1990, p. 33.)

The matter of bringing about a convergence of values and the appropriate use of moral agency by parents and their children is often accomplished through parental example and discipline. Of the latter, in the same address Elder Faust said: "One of the most difficult parental challenges is to appropriately discipline children. Child rearing is so individualistic. Every child is different and unique. What works with one may not work with another. I do not know who is wise enough to say what discipline is too harsh or what is too lenient except the parents of the children themselves, who love them most. It is a matter of prayerful discernment for the parents. Certainly the overarching and undergirding principle is that the discipline of children must be motivated more by love than by punishment." (P. 34.)

For many years I was perplexed by the scriptural edict: "I the Lord thy God am a jealous God, visiting the iniquity of the fathers upon the children unto the third and fourth generation of them that hate me" (Exodus 20:5; see also Exodus 34:7; Numbers 14:18; Deuteronomy 5:9; Mosiah 13:13). That scripture seems to infringe upon the moral agency of those born into the third and fourth generation. However, Elder Neal A. Maxwell offered some insight into this matter as he taught: "All are free to choose, of course, and we would not have it otherwise. Unfortunately, however, when some choose slackness, they are choosing not only for themselves, but for the next generation and the next. Small equivocations in parents can produce large deviations in their children! Earlier generations in a family may have reflected dedication, while some in the current generation evidence equivocation. Sadly, in the next, some may choose dissension as erosion takes its toll." ("Settle This in Your Hearts," *Ensign*, November 1992, p. 66.)

Rabbi Harold S. Kushner provided a further illustration into this process of transmitting sins into subsequent generations when he said: "Hell is the understanding that if I was sarcastic to my daughter when she was a little girl, she will be sarcastic to my grandchildren, and it will be my fault. Hell is the realization that every time I tell a lie because the truth is embarrassing, I am voting to make this a more deceitful world for my family to live in." ("The Human Soul's Quest for God," *Brigham Young Magazine*, February 1995, p. 28.)

It is a happy thought that not just bad habits but also traits of the divine nature can be transmitted into the third and fourth generation. In modern revelation the Lord revealed that when families and individuals within families develop patient and forgiving hearts toward those who offend them, "thou shalt be rewarded for thy righteousness; and also thy children and thy children's children unto the third and fourth generation" (D&C 98:30).

In the Book of Mormon the dramatic changes in the lives of Enos and Alma the Younger give hope to parents whose children were taught correct principles but who have taken time to observe how people of the world live their lives. Elder Boyd K. Packer quoted earlier Church leaders as he poignantly described the painful process of waiting for a prodigal to return, but he also provided a profound promise:

> It is not uncommon for responsible parents to lose one of their children, for a time, to influences over which they have no control. They agonize over rebellious sons or daughters. They are puzzled over why they are so helpless when they have tried so hard to do what they should.
>
> It is my conviction that those wicked influences one day will be overruled.
>
> "The Prophet Joseph Smith declared—and he never taught a more comforting doctrine—that the eternal sealing of faithful parents and the divine promises made to them for valiant service in the Cause of Truth, would save not only themselves, but likewise their posterity. Though some of the sheep may wander, the eye of the Shepherd is upon them, and sooner or later they will feel the tentacles of Divine Providence reaching out after them and drawing them back to the fold. Either in this life or the life to come, they will return. They will have to pay their debt to justice; they will suffer for their sins; and may tread a thorny path; but if it leads them at last, like the penitent Prodigal, to a loving and forgiving father's heart and home, the painful experience will not have been in vain. Pray for your careless and disobedient children; hold on to them with your faith. Hope on, trust on, till you see the salvation of God." (Orson F. Whitney, in Conference Report, April 1929, p. 110.)

We cannot overemphasize the value of temple marriage, the binding ties of the sealing ordinance, and the standards of worthiness required of them. When parents keep the covenants they have made at the altar of the temple, their children will be forever bound to them. President Brigham Young said:

"Let the father and mother, who are members of this Church and Kingdom, take a righteous course, and strive with all their might never to do a wrong, but to do good all their lives; if they have one child or one hundred children, if they conduct themselves towards them as they should, binding them to the Lord by their faith and prayers, I care not where those children go, they are bound up to their parents by an everlasting tie, and no power of earth or hell can separate them from their parents in eternity; they will return again to the fountain from whence they sprang." (*Discourses of Brigham Young,* sel. John A. Widtsoe [Salt Lake City: Deseret Book Co., 1941], p. 208.) ("Our Moral Environment," *Ensign,* May 1992, p. 68.)

Elder Howard W. Hunter provided some comforting reassurance to those who feel they have completely failed in their sacred responsibilities as parents:

A successful parent is one who has loved, one who has sacrificed, and one who has cared for, taught, and ministered to the needs of a child. If you have done all of these and your child is still wayward or troublesome or worldly, it could well be that you are, nevertheless, a successful parent. Perhaps there are children who have come into the world that would challenge any set of parents under any set of circumstances. Likewise, perhaps there are others who would bless the lives of, and be a joy to, almost any father or mother. ("Parents' Concern for Children," *Ensign,* November 1983, p. 65.)

Sometimes, even with the very best of intentions, we may try too hard to influence our children's lives at the very time we should be letting go. Some well-meaning parents make incursions upon their adult children's moral agency when they should be giving them opportunities to exercise their agency following the plan, discussed in the premortal council, that will lead to their growth and development. For instance, some parents and grandparents meddle in a couple's private decision regarding the desired number of children in their family. Still other parents adamantly insist that all their children live close by, sometimes engendering a tug-of-war between the family of the bride and the family of the groom.

There may also be the case of the father who has successfully established a family business enterprise with the hope of having his children take over the business some day. When each child in turn decides upon a career totally unrelated to the family business, some fathers graciously accept this use of their children's moral agency, but others cajole, bribe, and intimidate their offspring until their relationship suffers a permanent rift and alienation. Some children, not strong enough to stand on their own, accept their father's invitation, and this occasionally leads to a lifetime as a sort of indentured servant. There are, however, many happy examples of children who have willingly and anxiously accepted their loving father's tutorial preparation and have, indeed, assumed an important role in the family business, not only finding fulfillment in their careers but also developing a sacred bond with their fathers.

The point I wish to make is that youngsters must be taught correct principles and then be given the freedom to choose. I am not advocating anarchy or even a lessening of interest in our children's welfare, but there comes a time when we have to take off the training wheels and let them see if they can ride a bicycle without any help. Often this exercise will involve some falls, some bruises, and some skinned knees.

A colleague at an eastern university several years ago had always hoped that his children would follow in his footsteps as a university professor. But, alas, his youngest son had a consuming fascination for automobile engines. His highest aspiration in life was to become an automobile mechanic. Those of us who are less mechanically inclined tend to hold mechanics in very high esteem, especially when a car breaks down on the Nevada desert in the heat of summer. But my academic colleague suffered from the curse of respectability. He was terribly worried about what everyone would think about a professor's son who worked with his hands and got them very dirty each day.

I am pleased to report that the professor eventually overcame his reservations and actually began to develop an allowable degree of parental pride in his son's extraordinary talent in diagnosing automotive ailments. He was also pleased that his son could earn a good living and was extremely happy and settled in his chosen occupation.

The curse of respectability raises its head in other areas in which our children wish to use their agency in pursuing a course of action that breaks their parents' hearts such as by not going on a mission or not getting married in the temple. Ever since President Spencer W. Kimball challenged every young man to prepare to serve a full-time mission, there have been varying degrees of encouragement on the part of priesthood leaders and parents. The outcome has generally been favorable, as the number of missionaries reached President Kimball's initial goal of thirty thousand and is now hovering around fifty thousand missionaries.

As one who attributes much of his happiness in life to having served a mission, I have always enthusiastically endorsed President Kimball's counsel that every young man should serve a mission. But in some quarters extreme parental pressure is put upon a young man who is still struggling to obtain a testimony or with a problem that needs to be resolved. In certain instances a young man will indicate a willingness to serve a mission just to please his parents or his girlfriend. Some fathers promise to buy their sons a new car or to provide tuition at a preferred university at the conclusion of the mission. But unless this reason for serving is not soon replaced by loftier, holier motives, the mission experience can be a very trying one for companions, mission presidents, and especially for the missionary in question. How much better it is when we properly prepare our children for missions so they respond willingly and affirmatively to a mission call from the prophet! If they decide not to serve a mission, they still deserve the love of their parents.

Siblings, especially those who are older, can exert a great positive influence upon their brothers and sisters, but their potential to be a negative influence is also present. Denigrating nicknames, cynical responses, judgmental comments, and pervasive sarcasm can do much to destroy the self-image of a young adolescent already unsure of his or her identity. Such practices by older brothers and sisters in essence rob younger siblings of some of their moral agency. When children are convinced by others that they are stupid or clumsy it is unlikely that they will set their sights very high in life, and thus the range of their agency has been significantly curtailed.

Even the homes of righteous parents are not immune to "sible-war," as can be seen in the families of Adam and Eve, Jacob and his wives, and Lehi and Sariah.

Family patriarchs often have good intentions as to keeping their extended families together, but some of them fail to realize that their sons-in-law and daughters-in-law also have a set of parents and brothers and sisters. I know a fine man who prided himself in having all of his grandchildren come to his home for family home evening every Monday evening. He thought this practice was truly a little bit of heaven on earth. But soon some of the older grandchildren began to ask their parents why they could never have a family home evening of their own "with just the eight of us." This loving patriarch had unwittingly usurped the patriarchal role of his sons and sons-in-law. Moral agency is sometimes curbed even by the best intentions. This wise father and grandfather accepted the counsel of a few of his grandchildren who pointed out to him the need for doing a few things as a nuclear family without all the cousins.

As one who has several cousins who are really more like brothers and sisters, I would not wish to minimize the positive impact of extended families upon the lives of their members. When older cousins begin going on missions and getting married in the temple, it becomes the expected thing to do for younger cousins, and a wholesome family tradition develops which nurtures a legacy of faith for future generations.

Need for Counsel

Everyone can benefit from the advice from others, but sometimes those who are leaders assume that their role is to *give* advice, not *take* it. In some situations those who should provide advice to others are fearful to do so for a variety of reasons. Such was the case among President Harry S Truman's advisors during the outbreak of the Korean War in 1950. According to Richard Neustadt, an expert on the Truman administration, when the war began no one had calculated the costs of military involvement in defending South Korea. General MacArthur had made a hasty estimate that he could take two of his divisions from Japan and engage in an "early offensive action" which would adequately repel the North Koreans.

By the first of November 1950, however, the Chinese had intervened in the war with a large number of troops. Although they had not yet engaged the U.S. and U.N. forces in heated combat, President Truman's advisors feared for the security of MacArthur's meager forces. They agreed among themselves that MacArthur should be ordered to pull back and reduce the vulnerability of his troops. But according to Neustadt, "no one went to Truman, because everyone thought someone else should go." (Richard E. Neustadt, *Presidential Power* [New York: Wiley, 1960], p. 145.)

The generals and other military advisors deferred to the State Department, assuming that Secretary of State Dean Acheson "as guardian of 'policy'" should be the one to confront President Truman regarding a reversal of MacArthur's strategy. But Secretary Acheson was already under attack from several Congressmen, and he also had to tread lightly in his relationship with the Pentagon because of President Truman's high regard for the generals. Acheson assumed that the risks involved were primarily military; therefore, he felt justified to let the Joint Chiefs of Staff take a military initiative and suggest to Truman that MacArthur pull back his forces. (Ibid.)

In retrospect, Alexander George speculated that if Truman had received the advice he needed when he needed it and "had acted promptly, there would have been time to pull back MacArthur's forces before the Chinese launched their major offensive on November 28. The catastrophe that followed might have been avoided altogether or greatly reduced." ("Adaptation to Stress in Political Decision Making: The Individual, Small Group, and Organizational Contexts," in George V. Coelho, David A. Hamburg, and John E. Adams, eds., *Coping and Adaptation* [New York: Basic Books, Inc., 1974], p. 227.)

Safety in Counsel

Some of the most pleasant and painful experiences in our lives occur in the process of bringing about a coherence and convergence of several different perspectives. Callings within the Church are especially suited as the Lord's laboratory for helping to "perfect the Saints" and helping them to acquire the attributes of godliness. Whenever we live or work in close proximity to others it is virtually inevitable that there will be an occasional divergence of opinion that requires tolerance, patience, compassion, kindness, and forgiveness.

A great source of strength in the Church is the council system, in which presidents and their counselors preside over committees and councils. The merging of minds in a presidency or committee or council requires us to subordinate our personal preferences for the good of the whole, and the resulting decisions are generally more sound than those made by only one person. We would do well to remember a great principle taught in Proverbs: "Where no counsel is, the people fall: but in the multitude of counsellors there is safety" (Proverbs 11:14). It takes longer to make a decision when several people are involved than when we make a decision alone. But when others are involved they serve as an error-correction mechanism. Others see the blind spots that elude our own view of a given problem.

We gain valuable insight from the Book of Abraham with regard to the council held to discuss the creation of the earth:

> And the Gods took counsel among themselves and said: Let us go down and form man in our image, after our likeness.
>
> And the Gods said among themselves: On the seventh time we will end our work, which we have counseled; and we will rest on the seventh time from all our work which we have counseled. (Abraham 4:26; 5:2.)

Notwithstanding His omniscience and omnipotence, our Heavenly Father counseled with the other Gods. Can we as mortal women and men do any less than to counsel with those around us, with our children, with our spouses, and with all those with whom we labor in the Church?

When I was a young boy it was not a regular practice in our family to hold family councils. However, I do remember one momentous occasion when a council was held to discuss a very important matter—the naming of our newly arrived baby sister. The council was convened and the agenda was outlined. I served as scribe. My parents had recently seen the movie *Cyrano de Bergerac*, and my father was in favor of the name Roxanne, the heroine of the movie. The rest of us leaned toward the name Nancy. The options were openly discussed, and with a sense of anticipation in the air the ballots were cast. Notwithstanding my father's patriarchal position in the family, he acceded to the family vote and gave our little sister the name of Nancy.

Another family found great strength in the council system as the father was suddenly informed that he would be laid off from his place of employment. Sauntering home with feelings of dejection and low self-esteem, he reluctantly called the family together to break the news. As this humble father explained the economic plight to his family, each in turn came forth with valuable suggestions regarding how they could make ends meet until he was gainfully employed again. Each of the children expressed a willingness to forego a long-anticipated vacation, and they volunteered to curtail many of their normal recreational activities.

The older children who had part-time jobs volunteered to contribute their earnings to a family financial pool, and the younger children volunteered to get odd jobs to help as best they could. The family went down to the basement and inventoried their supply of food. It became apparent that, as long as they did not have to have meat for every meal, there would plenty of freeze-dried vegetables, powdered eggs and potatoes, bottled fruit, rice, beans, pasta, and flour to provide nutritious meals for the family for several months to come.

This humble family concluded their family council with a kneeling family prayer, and with tears streaming down each face they felt the confirmation of the Spirit that "all is well, all is well." That night, instead of going to bed depressed, that unemployed father retired to bed with a heart filled with gratitude for his eternal family. In the multitude of counselors there was safety.

Law of Common Consent

I have been blessed many times with an assignment from the President of the Council of the Twelve to organize a new stake or to reorganize a stake presidency. In such an experience, after praying for inspiration and guidance an Area Authority and I begin interviewing several brethren whom the stake president and his counselors have arranged for us to meet.

I remember an occasion in which, as we interviewed one particular brother, a very warm and impressive feeling came into both my heart and the heart of the Area Authority. The confirmation of the Spirit was clear and unmistakable that this man was to be the next stake president. After interviewing his wife and extending the call to him we gave him some time to prayerfully select his counselors. The next morning we presented their names to the entire congregation.

The voting was unanimous in the affirmative. We call this the law of common consent. This was not a majority vote as part of a democratic political process, but rather a physical manifestation signified by the raised hand that every member of that congregation believed "that a man must be called of God, by prophecy, and by the laying on of hands by those who are in authority, to preach the Gospel and administer in the ordinances thereof" (Articles of Faith 1:5).

The outgoing stake presidency were men with a combined experience of over two dozen years service in a stake presidency. They were in their mid-fifties, men of wisdom and sound judgment and experience. They were replaced by men in their early forties with no experience in a stake presidency, but it was readily apparent from the outpouring of love and support they received that the members of that particular stake fully realized that the Church is organized "for the perfecting of the saints" (Ephesians 4:12).

In His infinite wisdom the Lord calls His servants through divine inspiration. Sometimes those servants are fishermen and carpenters and sometimes they are lawyers and doctors. Sometimes the most obvious man in the ward is *not* called to be the bishop, so that he may continue learning humility and the one who *is* called may become perfected enough to receive inspiration and guidance for the entire ward.

The law of common consent is part of the invisible glue that binds members of the Church to their leaders. Wherever we happen to live we may often be better prepared than those with whom we serve, and there may at times be an Oliver Cowdery inclination to reject the counsel of others. But as we are called to serve as counselors and on councils and committees it is well to remember the Lord's injunction to the presiding quorums of the Church that "every decision made by either of these quorums must be by the unanimous voice of the same" . . .[or] "their decisions are not entitled to the same blessings" (D&C 107:27–29).

Any one of us may well be the brightest person in the bishopric or the Young Women presidency or the high council, but unless and until we subordinate our will to the law of common consent and are willing to receive counsel as well as to give counsel, and are willing to concede and compromise and obtain consensus, then our potential influence for good will be greatly limited. True joy and happiness in our respective Church callings can be ours when we cheerfully and wholeheartedly sustain our leaders and yield our hearts to God.

The Goldilocks Syndrome

That favorite fairy tale by Jakob and Wilhelm Grimm, "Goldilocks and the Three Bears," serves as a suitable illustration of some of the challenges and concerns that arise from the collective convergence of moral agency among married couples, members of a family, a group, a council, or a committee. As a youngster, I considered Goldilocks to be a person of heroic stature. She was courageous and curious and lived a life filled with adventure and intrigue. And when in danger she could run fast. Now, with the passage of time, I reflect upon all the "Goldilocks types" I have known in my life, and I have grown to realize that the Goldilocks syndrome can make life rather unhappy for others.

Mission presidents inherit more than a few young men and women who have grown up in parental households where the food was never too hot or never too cold, but always *just* right. The beds were never too hard and never too soft, but always *just* right. Then Goldilocks arrives in the mission field where people eat raw fish for breakfast, sleep on a straw mat on the floor, and stamp out cockroaches for recreation. Life takes on a new dimension requiring increased tolerance and the subordination of personal preferences for the good of the kingdom.

And what about members of presidencies, committees, councils—or, for that matter, members of families? Do we, like
Goldilocks, always hold fast to *our* own personal preferences and
point of view by ignoring the preferences of others because they are
"too hot" or "too cold" or "too hard" or "too soft"? Is there a little
bit of Professor Henry Higgins in all of us, each wondering why
others cannot be like us?

And how is a collective convergence of moral agency reached
whereby men and women of goodwill arrive at a unanimous decision? The Lord provides the pattern, which is just as applicable to
marriage and family relationships as it is to bishoprics, stake presidencies, and priesthood quorums: "The decision of these quorums,
or either of them, are to be made in all . . . lowliness of heart, meekness and long suffering, and in faith, and virtue, and knowledge,
temperance, patience, godliness, brotherly kindness and charity"
(D&C 107:30).

President Ezra Taft Benson aptly observed: "Pride is concerned
with *who* is right. Humility is concerned with *what* is right." What
is right is that, while we treasure our own moral agency, we are also
sensitive to the agency of others so that ofttimes it becomes more
important to be unified than to be dominant. When eternal principles are involved we should, of course, defend those principles.
But often the issue at hand is not one of principle but rather one of
personal preference. It is then that the collective convergence of
moral agency can reflect the Savior's example in deferring to His
Father: "I do always those things that please him" (John 8:29).

President Harold B. Lee aptly observed: "There is no limit to
what we can accomplish if we are not concerned with who gets the
credit." As men and women of good will strive to do the will of the
Father, their personal preferences will generally converge to the
satisfaction and blessing of all.

Nevertheless they did fast and pray oft, and did wax stronger and stronger in their humility, and firmer and firmer in the faith of Christ, unto the filling their souls with joy and consolation, yea, even to the purifying and the sanctification of their hearts, which sanctification cometh because of their yielding their hearts unto God (Helaman 3:35). ✍

Chapter Seven

Yielding Our Hearts to God

Amaleki, an ancient Nephite prophet, exhorted the Saints of his day to offer their whole souls as an offering unto Christ, the Holy One of Israel (see Omni 1:26). The language in his invitation to come unto Christ is not coincidental. He spoke not of token donations of our time and means and talents, but of offering our whole souls to Christ. Ofttimes it is much easier to sacrifice our financial resources and our time than it is to sacrifice our sins. This point was not lost on the father of King Lamoni, who, notwithstanding his wealth and power, prayed to God that "I will give away all my sins to know thee, and that I may be raised from the dead, and be saved at the last day" (Alma 22:18).

A Lesson from Oliver Cowdery

Yielding our hearts to God has many dimensions in addition to our willingness to sacrifice our sins and our resources. Sometimes it requires sacrificing our pride. In October of 1834, Oliver Cowdery eloquently recounted the great spiritual experience he had while serving as Joseph's scribe: "These were days never to be forgotten— to sit under the sound of a voice dictated by the inspiration of heaven, awakened the utmost gratitude of this bosom! Day after day I continued, uninterrupted, to write from his mouth, as he translated with the Urim and Thummim . . . the history or record called 'The Book of Mormon.'" (Joseph Smith—History 1:71, footnote.)

Continuing, Oliver described the ecstatic joy which filled their hearts as the resurrected John the Baptist conferred the Aaronic Priesthood upon Joseph and himself.

Joseph's confidence in and reliance upon Oliver is reflected by the fact that in February of 1835 the Prophet invited Oliver to give the newly called Council of the Twelve their apostolic charge. Among other excellent counsel, Oliver admonished them to "cultivate great humility; for I know the pride of the human heart" (*History of the Church* 2:195).

In April of 1836 Oliver was in the Kirtland Temple with the Prophet when they "saw the Lord standing upon the breastwork of the pulpit" and subsequently Moses, Elias, and Elijah restored priesthood keys to them (see D&C 110).

But just two years later Oliver was invited to appear before a disciplinary council to be tried for his membership in the Church. Among the charges was the allegation that he had persecuted the brethren through urging lawsuits against them. It was also alleged that he had defamed the character of the Prophet and that he had treated "the Church with contempt by not attending meetings." It was further alleged that he had forsaken his calling "appointed him by revelation, for the sake of filthy lucre, and turning to the practice of law." (*History of the Church* 3:16–17.)

Oliver refused to attend the disciplinary council and to face his brethren, but he did send a letter to Bishop Edward Partridge in response to the charges made against him. Note the change in this man who, in humbler days, had enthusiastically served as the

Prophet's scribe. Note the justification of his behavior and his arrogant attitude as he wrote the following:

> My venerable ancestor was among the little band, who landed on the rocks of Plymouth in 1620—with him he brought those maxims, and a body of those laws which were the result and experience of many centuries, on the basis of which now stands our great and happy government; and they are so interwoven in my nature, have so long been inculcated into my mind by a liberal and intelligent ancestry that I am wholly unwilling to exchange them for anything less liberal, less benevolent, or less free.
>
> . . . This attempt to control me in my temporal interests, I conceive to be a disposition to take from me a portion of my Constitutional privileges and inherent right—I only, respectfully, ask leave, therefore, to withdraw from a society assuming they have such right. (*History of the Church* 3:18.)

Oliver had been a man of great native intellect, eloquent speech, and unflinching loyalty to the Prophet as he served as Second Elder of the Church and later as Assistant President of the Church. And now he had discarded the blessings of the gospel and membership in the Church because he refused to accept the counsel of others.

Let it be said to Oliver's credit that, although he did not live long enough after his reinstatement to rejoin the Saints in the Salt Lake Valley, a decade after his excommunication he was rebaptized and returned to full fellowship in the Church, never having denied his testimony of the Book of Mormon.

He Must Increase, but I Must Decrease

A paragon example of one who yielded his heart unto Christ was John the Baptist. One day as his father, Zacharias, was officiating in the temple the angel Gabriel appeared to him and announced that his wife, Elisabeth, would bear a son and that he should be called John (see Luke 1:13). The angel then declared that this precious son would have a very special mission "to make ready a people prepared for the Lord" (Luke 1:17).

Six months after Elisabeth's conception, "the angel Gabriel was sent from God . . . to a virgin . . . [whose] name was Mary [declaring to her:] blessed art thou among women. . . for thou hast found favour with God. And, behold, thou shalt conceive in thy womb, and bring forth a son, and shalt call his name JESUS." (Luke 1:26–31.)

Shortly thereafter, Mary "went into the hill country" of Judah to visit her cousin Elisabeth. As Mary entered the house and Elisabeth heard her greeting, Elisabeth's babe leaped within her womb and she declared: "Blessed art thou among women, and blessed is the fruit of thy womb. And whence is this to me, that the mother of my Lord should come to me?" Mary responded: "My soul doth magnify the Lord." Mary stayed with her cousin for about three months and then returned home to Nazareth. (Luke 1:39–56.)

In the Doctrine and Covenants we learn that after John was born "he was baptized while he was yet in his childhood, and was ordained by the angel of God at the time he was eight days old unto this power . . . to make straight the way of the Lord" (D&C 84:28).

The Prophet Joseph Smith taught:

When Herod's edict went forth to destroy the young children, John was about six months older than Jesus, and came under this hellish edict, and Zacharias caused his mother to take him into the mountains, where he was raised on locusts and wild honey. When his father refused to disclose his hiding place, and being the officiating high priest at the Temple that year, [he] was slain by Herod's order, between the porch and the altar, as Jesus said. (*Teachings of the Prophet Joseph Smith*, sel. Joseph Fielding Smith [Deseret Book Co., 1976], p. 261.)

From the Prophet's teachings, we now understand the context of John's declaration when he said, "I am the voice of one crying in the wilderness, Make straight the way of the Lord" (John 1:23). In the process of preparing the way, John acquired many devoted disciples. In addition to baptizing them, he taught his disciples how to pray (see Luke 11:1) and also the importance of fasting (Matthew 9:14). But in all of his teaching, John invariably pointed his disciples toward the coming of the Savior, such as when he told them: "I indeed baptize you with water unto repentance: but he that cometh after me is mightier than I, whose shoes I am not worthy to bear: he shall baptize you with the Holy Ghost, and with fire" (Matthew 3:11).

Early in his own ministry the Savior extolled the preparatory work of John the Baptist, declaring that "among those that are born of women there is not a greater prophet than John the Baptist" (Luke 7:28). The LDS Bible Dictionary informs us that John's "ministry has operated in three dispensations: he was the last of the prophets under the law of Moses, he was the first of the New Testament prophets, and he brought the Aaronic Priesthood to the dispensation of the fulness of times" (p. 715).

John clearly understood his mission as a forerunner to the Savior whose calling it was "to make ready a people prepared for the Lord" (Luke 1:17). After he had baptized the Savior, John continued "baptizing in Aenon near to Salim" (John 3:23), and some of John's disciples became concerned that others were being baptized by the disciples of Jesus and that so many people were beginning to follow Jesus (see John 3:23–26; 4:1–2).

The meekness and humility of John and his unqualified devotion to the Savior are reflected in his spiritually mature response to his overly concerned followers: "He must increase, but I must decrease" (John 3:30). And so it is in each of our lives. If we are to become true disciples of the Savior, *He* must increase, but *we* must decrease.

Becoming Prisoners of Christ

It was the young Saul of Tarsus who looked after the clothes of those involved in the stoning of Stephen (Acts 7:58). Thereafter Saul pursued a zealous career of making "havoc of the church," frequently punishing the Saints "in every synagogue," and assenting to their imprisonment and death (Acts 8:3; 26:10–11). His fanatical "threatenings and slaughter against the disciples of the Lord" struck great fear in the hearts of the Church members (Acts 9:1).

And then, on the road to Damascus, he had a dramatic spiritual experience that would forever change his life. He later wrote to the Galatians that after his conversion he went into the Arabian desert, and "then after three years," he finally "went up to Jerusalem to see Peter," who was the President of the Church (Galatians 1:16–18).

As Saul of Tarsus began his mission he took his Latin name Paul and turned his life to Christ. On several different occasions the Apostle Paul referred to himself as "a prisoner of Christ" (Ephesians 3:1; see also 4:1; 2 Timothy 1:8; Philemon 1:1, 9, 23). Once he had made the decision to serve the Lord, that decision was irrevocable.

Borrowing a parable from George Macdonald, C. S. Lewis eloquently described the often painful process of striving for perfection, a process with which the Apostle Paul became very familiar throughout his life:

> Imagine yourself as a living house. God comes in to rebuild that house. At first, perhaps, you can understand what He is doing. He is getting the drains right and stopping the leaks in the roof and so on: you knew that those jobs needed doing and so you are not surprised. But presently he starts knocking the house about in a way that hurts abominably and does not seem to make sense. What on earth is He up to? The explanation is that He is building quite a different house from the one you thought of—throwing out a new wing here, putting on an extra floor there, running up towers, making courtyards. You thought you were going to be made into a decent little cottage: but He is building a palace. He intends to come and live in it Himself. (C.S. Lewis, *Mere Christianity* [New York: MacMillan Publishing Co., Inc., 1952], p. 174.)

After a previous life of resistance, Paul yielded to the Great Builder's plan. Paul's frequent use of the term "prisoner of Christ" is significant, for he was very familiar with prisons and prisoners. Before his conversion he had personally sent numerous Saints to prison (see Acts 26:10), and after his conversion he himself had been forcibly committed to prison (Acts 23:10–11; 28:17–18). He had observed firsthand the restricted latitude of free will in the lives of other prisoners and had experienced this confinement in his own life when imprisoned.

Thus, when he confesses that *he* has become a willing prisoner of Christ, he reveals that he has surrendered his moral agency to Christ and that his only desire is to do the will of the Lord.

As Paul became Christ's prisoner, his life began to more closely approximate the Savior's life and the Savior's relationship with His Father. Myriad scriptures could be cited to describe this relationship, but let us review only a few of them in headline form.

After healing at the pool of Bethesda the man who had suffered an infirmity for thirty-eight years, the Savior humbly declared, "The Son can do nothing of himself, but what he seeth the Father do" (John 5:19). He later added: "I seek not mine own will, but the will of the Father which hath sent me" (John 5:30).

As He taught in the temple, the Savior reiterated that "I do nothing of myself; but as my Father hath taught me. . . . I do always those things that please him." (John 8:28–29; see also John 4:34; 6:38; 7:17.)

The prophet Abinadi foresaw the Savior's earthly ministry, during which time He would "be led, crucified, and slain, the flesh becoming subject even unto death, the will of the Son being swallowed up in the will of the Father" (Mosiah 15:7). What an eloquent description of what it means to be truly obedient: "the will of the Son being swallowed up in the will of the Father."

And then that fateful hour arrived as the Savior began to atone for our sins in the Garden of Gethsemane. The weight of your sins and mine caused Him to bleed from every pore and moved Him to plead: "Father, if thou be willing, remove this cup from me: nevertheless not my will, but thine, be done" (Luke 22:42).

Inherent in each of these scriptures, and countless others, is the fact that the Savior's entire life reflected His humility and meekness in subordinating His will to the will of His Father.

The Anti-Nephi-Lehies

After Alma the Younger and the four sons of King Mosiah—Ammon, Aaron, Omner, and Himni—were confronted by an angel of the Lord and had forsaken their wicked ways, "they could not bear that any human soul should perish" (Mosiah 28:3). This spiritual urgency with which they preached the gospel was instrumental in converting thousands of Lamanites to a knowledge of the truth. To acknowledge their complete conversion and to distinguish themselves from the unbelievers, these righteous converts called themselves Anti-Nephi-Lehies. (See Alma 23.)

They had previously been a warmongering people who delighted in bloodshed, but after they yielded their hearts to God they
buried their weapons of war "deep in the earth" as a testimony to
God that they had, indeed, undergone a mighty change of heart
and had no more disposition to do evil (see Alma 24).

Following Nephi's counsel to "liken all scriptures unto us," we
can use the conversion of the Anti-Nephi-Lehies as a metaphor for
our own lives. When we become truly converted, the testimony of
our conversion may well be borne in our burying deep in the earth
our sharp tongues in lieu of sharp swords. Our post-conversion san-
itary landfill might also be used to discard our hot tempers, our evil
speech patterns, our penchant for off-color jokes, our ethnic epi-
thets, our greediness, unkindness, and lack of compassion.

As we bury deep within the earth those satanic inclinations
that impair our becoming partakers of the divine nature, we, like
John the Baptist, can demonstrate to a loving and patient
Heavenly Father that the Savior's life pattern is continually
increasing in importance in our lives.

Charles C. Rich

The spirit of "thy will be done" was strongly reflected in the life
of Elder Charles C. Rich. Brother Rich was ordained an Apostle in
1849 at the age of 39 after serving as a general in the Mormon
Battalion. Two years later Elder Rich was called to settle San
Bernardino, California. Then in 1863 President Brigham Young
asked Elder Rich to establish a settlement in the Bear Lake Valley
in what is now southeastern Idaho.

In June of 1864 the entire Rich family joined a band of nearly
a thousand residents at Bear Lake and began constructing log houses with roofs comprised of "a layer of willow branches, then a cov-
ering of straw topped off with thick sod" (Leonard J. Arrington,
Charles C. Rich [Provo, Utah: Brigham Young University, 1974], p.
261). That first summer Brother Rich proposed that the Saints celebrate the Fourth of July in grand style with a homemade flag, a
little brass band, and lots of dancing.

But the joy of the occasion was short-lived. The very next day
frost killed the spring wheat and stunted the growth of corn. The

subsequent winter was extremely bitter, and the potatoes and wheat froze because of lack of storage facilities. The John Clifton family grew so short of supplies that their children "were kept in bed to conserve their strength." (Ibid., p. 263.)

As the individual and collective misery of the Saints increased, murmuring was heard in their ranks and some of the brethren asked for a meeting with Brother Rich to discuss the possibility of abandoning the settlement for a more hospitable environment elsewhere. Elder Rich, sensing their concerns even before they were expressed, rose to his feet, and addressed those in attendance:

> In the fall of 1863 President Young called me into his office and said, "Brother Rich, I want you to go up to Bear Lake Valley and see if it can be opened for settlement; and if it can, I want that you should take a company there and settle it."
>
> That was all I needed. It was a call. I came up here, with a few brethren; we looked over the valley; and, although the altitude was high, the snows heavy, and frosts severe, there was plenty of water for irrigation purposes and plenty of fish in the lake and streams. So, with a company, I came here and settled with my family.
>
> There have been many hardships. That I admit. . . and these we have shared together. But if you want to go somewhere else, that is your right, and I do not want to deprive you of it. If you are of a mind to leave here, my blessing will go with you. But I must stay here, even if I stay alone. President Young called me here, and here I will remain till he releases me and gives me leave to go. (Ibid., p. 264.)

Elder Charles C. Rich, Mormon general, western frontiersman, Apostle of the Lord, and prisoner of Jesus Christ, died nineteen years later in the Bear Lake Valley at Paris, Idaho, on November 17, 1883. He claimed the blessings of the Book of Mormon promised to those who yield "their hearts unto God" (Helaman 3:35).

The late Rex E. Lee is another example of one who yielded his heart to God. Notwithstanding very serious and persistent health challenges, he accepted the call of the Brethren to serve as the President of Brigham Young University. In spite of his weakness, he performed a meritorious service and relinquished the reins of leadership only a few weeks before his passing.

Young people and elderly couples yield their hearts to God

when they accept mission calls to faraway places. They kiss their loved ones goodbye, leave their homes, and follow Peter's admonition to "be ready always to give an answer to every man that asketh you a reason of the hope that is in you with meekness and fear" (1 Peter 3:15).

Each year at the Missionary Training Center in Provo, Utah, more than a hundred newly called mission presidents and their wives gather at the feet of prophets, seers, and revelators to learn how to fulfill their sacred challenging duties. It is one thing to be called to be bishop or stake Relief Society president and be allowed to stay in your own home and be with all your children, neighbors, and loved ones. It is quite another challenge to be called to interrupt one's professional career for three years, (often with no guarantee of job re-entry), to disrupt one's family by taking some of the children and leaving others behind, and to abandon one's house and neighborhood. But these faithful Saints accept the invitation of the First Presidency, and they yield their hearts to God.

Sometimes yielding our hearts to God requires us to let go when a loved one is in the throes of a critical illness or the victim of a serious accident. After priesthood blessings and pleading prayers, it wrenches our soul to let go of a three-year-old who lies in a coma following an automobile accident. It tugs at our heartstrings to let go of a vivacious teenager who has contracted a terminal illness. It is difficult to bid farewell to a loving middle-aged mother who will leave behind a family of young children. It is also a challenge to let go of loving grandparents who have valiantly fulfilled their missions on earth. But if we are to become like the Savior, then we too must yield our hearts to God and be willing to declare: "Not my will, but thine be done."

There are many actions in our daily lives which can reflect the degree to which we are willing to accept Father's divine will. For example, men and women who receive their temple endowments yet persist in wearing immodest clothing have not yielded their hearts to God, nor have those who wish to negotiate a narrow meaning of an honest tithe, or who press their bishop for a broad definition of the Word of Wisdom during a temple interview. Those who have truly yielded their hearts to God need no lengthy instructions regarding modesty, tithing, the Word of Wisdom, or keeping the Sabbath day holy.

Robert Robinson and John Wyeth have aptly captured the essence of yielding our hearts unto God in that grand old hymn, "Come, Thou Fount of Every Blessing."

> O to grace how great a debtor
> Daily I'm constrained to be!
> Let thy goodness, as a fetter,
> Bind my wandering heart to thee.
> Prone to wander, Lord, I feel it,
> Prone to leave the God I love;
> Here's my heart, O take and seal it;
> Seal it for thy courts above.
> > (*Hymns* [1948], no. 70.)

May each of us live our lives in the spirit of "not my will but *thine* be done," which the Savior exemplified throughout His earthly ministry, that we too may use our God-given moral agency in yielding our hearts to God.

Index

— A —

Aaron, 139
Aaronic Priesthood. *See* Priesthood
Abinadi, 51, 139
Abortion, 46, 50
Abuse, 92, 107
  healing from, 104–5
  sexual, 100–101
  story, 93
Accountability, 10, 35, 97
Acheson, Dean, 127
Adam, 5
Addiction, 12–16, 35, 46, 54, 66,
  87, 89, 100, 107
Administration to the sick, 68
Advice. *See* Counsel
Afflictions. *See* Opposition
Agency, and addiction, 12–16
  and angels, 65
  and arrogance, 21–24

colloquial expressions of, 3–4
and common choices, 111
and debt, 16–17
and discouragement, 17–21
and the Fall, 5–6
and family life, 115–26
gift of, 5
and ingratitude, 32–34
and living in the past, 39–40
and marriage, 110–13
and the premortal council, 4, 6
price of, 7–9
and public interviews, 96–97
restricted, 4
and rumor, 24–26
and shifting responsibility, 35–39
surrendering of, to others, 1–3, 89
Airplane, couple on (story), 15–16
Alcohol addiction, 14, 54, 87, 100
Alcoholics Anonymous (AA), 94
Alder, Valdean, 72–73

Alma the Elder, on baptism, 85
   prayed for son, 65
Alma the Younger, angel appeared
   to, 65, 139
   conversion of, 122
   and Corianton, 36
   father prayed for, 65
   on his conversion, 40
   and Korihor, 22
   on law of Moses, 51
   "wickedness never was happi-
   ness," 8, 94
Amaleki, 133
American Medical Association,
   101, 102
American Psychiatric Association,
   101
Ammon, 105–6, 139
Angel(s), 72
   and agency, 65
   appeared to Alma the Younger,
   65, 139
   appeared to Paul, 65
   appeared to Zacharias, 13
Anger, 2
Anna Karenina (novel), 39–40, 49
Anorexia, 107
Anti-Christ, 22
Anti-Nephi-Lehies, 105–6, 139–40
Arrogance, 21–24
   See also Pride
Asay, Carlos, 30
Asch, Solomon E., 96
Ashley, Utah, 83
Atonement. *See* Jesus Christ
Australian family (story), 69
Austria, 113

— B —

Baal, 43, 47
Ballard, M. Russell, on prayer, 66,
   99

Baptism, 68
Barabbas, 42
Barnabas, 50
Bavarian Alps, 113
Bear Lake Valley, Idaho, 140–41
Beatitudes. *See* Sermon on the
   Mount
Beer drinking, 46
Benjamin. *See* King Benjamin
Benson, Ezra Taft, on home teach-
   ing, 86
   on patriarchal blessings, 72
   on pride, 132
   on right of choice, 4
Bishops, 94
Blame. *See* Responsibility
Blessing of infants, 68
Blessing of the sick, 68
Blessings, claiming of, 75–76
Bombeck, Erma, on shopping, 110
Book of Mormon, 5, 71, 107, 134,
   135
Bradford, William R., "chasing
   parked cars," 11
Brass plates, 81
Bridge collapse (story), 69
Brigham Young University, 45, 53,
   141
Brother of Jared, 80
Bulimia, 107
Burn victim (story), 30–31
BYU Motion Picture Studio, 28

— C —

Caesarea, 53
Caffeine, 54
Caleb, 78
Canaan, 78
Career choices, 77–78
Carnival (story), 19–20
Celestial kingdom, 21
Charity, 18–19, 21, 31, 63

Chastity, 50, 112
Chesterton, G. K., on arrogance, 22
Children, and agency, 115–26
  and gratitude, 34
  individuality of, 117
  responsibility for, 38
  wayward, 122–23
China, 127
Churchill, Winston, 56
Church Music Committee, 56
Cigarettes. See Tobacco addiction
Clark, J. Reuben, on interest, 16
Clifton, John, 141
Collective action, 39
Colton, Philander, 83
Colton, Polly Matilda Merrill, 83
"Come, Thou Fount of Every
    Blessing" (hymn), 143
Comforter, the. See Holy Ghost
Commandments, 32
Common consent, law of, 129–31
Commons, 37–38
Compassion, 128
Compromise, 112
Condie, Craig, 29, 109–10
Condie, Dorothea, 115
Confession, 90–95
Conformity, 59
Consecration, 22, 59
Constitution of the Church, 86
Conversion, 40, 52, 106, 137–38,
    139–40
Copenhagen, 15
Corianton, 36
Cornelius, 52–53
Council system, 127–29
Counsel, need for, 126–27
Counseling, 2–3, 98–100, 105, 107,
    108
  and hypnosis, 100–102
  and support groups, 87–100
  and trust, 103–4
"Counselitis," 98–100

Covenants, 59, 67
Cowdery, Oliver, 78, 131, 134–35
Creation, 128
Cultural traditions, 36, 48–59
Customs. See Cultural traditions
Cyrano de Bergerac (movie), 129

— D —

Dating, 50
Dead Sea, 102–3
Debt, 16–17
Decision-making strategy, 76–84
DeGaulle, Charles, 56
Delilah, 112
Depression (financial), 26
Depression (mental), 21
Despair, 34
Devil. See Satan
Differences. See Opposition
Discernment, 97
Discipline, 118–21
Discouragement, 17–21
Disobedience, 32
Divorce, 99–100, 112
DNA, 110
Doolittle, Eliza, 111
Doumas, Marty, 30–31
Drug addiction, 14, 87, 89, 107

— E —

Eating addiction, 12
Edison, Thomas Alva, 54, 79–80
Edmunds, Mary Ellen, on spending
    money, 17
Education, 22–24
Eli, 55, 119
Elias, 134
Elijah, 43, 47, 134
Elisabeth (musical), 113–14
Elisabeth (wife of Zacharias),
    135–36

Endangered American Dream, The
  (book), 13
Endowment (ordinance), 15, 68, 142
Endurance, 9
England, 37
Enos, 122
Erikson, Kai, on trauma, 27, 105
Ether, on the Holy Ghost, 63
Ethnic stereotypes, 36
Evans, Richard L., on price of
  agency, 9
Eve, 5
Ezekiel, on living waters, 102

— F —

Faith. *See* Jesus Christ
Fall, the, 5–6
"False memory syndrome," 101–2
Family, contention in, 125–26
  councils, 129
  extended, 126
  and "false memory syndrome,"
    101–2
  forsaking, 55
  is like a symphony, 116–17
  life, 78, 110, 115–26
  love of, 55
  prayer, 69–70, 129
  relationships, 13
  transmitting traits through,
    121–22
Family history, 55
Fasting, 66–67
Father in Heaven. *See* Heavenly
  Father
Faust, James E., on family prayer,
  69–70
  on parenting, 118, 120–21
  on patriarchal blessings, 72
Featherstone, Vaughn J, on
  Humpty Dumpty, 66–67
Ferris wheel (story), 19–20

Feuding, 26–28
Finances, 16–17
Fire (story), 30–31
Flood (story), 34
Football, 80
Football game (story), 29–30
Forgiveness, 7, 26–32, 44, 94, 105,
  107, 112, 128
  collective, 105
France, drinking in, 46
Frankfurt, 15
Frankl, Viktor, "survival for what?,"
  12
Franz-Joseph, Emperor, 113
Free agency. *See* Agency
"Free-rider tendency," 37
French hymns, 56

— G —

Gabriel, 135–36
Gambling, 12
Garden of Eden, 5
Gardner, John W., on traditions,
  48–49
Gender differences, 112
Genealogy, 55
General Authorities, 23–24, 68–69
Genetics, 110
Gentiles, 51–53
Geophagy, 12
George, Alexander, 127
German armies, 106
Germany, drinking in, 46
Gethsemane, 65, 139
Gift-giving, to oneself, 13
Godly sorrow, 94–95
God the Father. *See* Heavenly
  Father
Goldilocks syndrome, 131–32
Good Samaritan, 39
Gossip. *See* Rumor
Gossip (poem), 25

Grace, 9
Grand Council. *See* premortal
   council
Gratitude, 20, 22, 32–34
Great Depression, 26
Grievances. *See* Feuding
Grimm, Jakob and Wilhelm,
   "Goldilocks and the Three
   Bears," 131
Group therapy, 86–100
Grudges. *See* Unforgiving hearts
Guerrilla warfare, 24, 26

— H —

Happiness, 8, 16, 17, 33, 107
Hardin, Garrett, "The Tragedy of
   the Commons," 37–38
Hatfield and McCoy clans, 27
Healing, and living waters, 102–3
   Lord's pattern of, 104–7
   and service, 107–8
Hearts, unforgiving. *See*
   Unforgiving hearts
Heavenly Father, awareness of, 38
   and healing, 104–5
   moral agency is gift from, 7
   at premortal council, 4, 6
   provides resources, 62
Helaman, on happiness and
   iniquity, 8
Hickman, Martin B., 111
Higgins, Henry, 111, 132
High blood pressure, 21
Himni, 139
Hinckley, Gordon B., on pornography, 13–14
   on war on earth, 61–62
Holy Ghost, confirmation by, 130
   to the Gentiles, 51
   gift of the, 53, 63–64
   gifts from the, 72
   quickens minds, 33

   seal of the, 83
   speaking by the, 68
Home teaching, 72–75, 86, 117–18
Homosexuality, 87, 89, 107
Hoover, Herbert, 26
Hope, 21
Houses, debt for, 17
Howe, Steve, 35
Humility, 21, 112, 132, 134, 137,
   139
Humpty Dumpty (nursery rhyme),
   66–67
Hunter, Howard W., on blessings,
   76
   on parenting, 123
Hymns, 56–57
Hypnotherapy, 100–102
Hypocrisy, 22

— I —

Idaho, 140–41
"I Just Belong to Me" (song),
   113–14
Impatience, 87
India, 17
Individuality, 117
"I Need Thee Every Hour" (hymn),
   57
Ingratitude, 32–34
In-laws, 114–15
Institute program, 45
Intelligence, 22–24
Internet, 12, 13
Interviews, 95–96
   public, 96–97
Intolerance, 87
Iowa couple (story), 15–16
Isabel, 36
Isaiah, "evil good and good evil," 43
   on fasting, 66
   on spending money, 78
   "swallow up death," 108

Italian customs, 55
Italian Saints, 56

— J —

Jacob (son of Lehi), on counseling
    the Lord, 66
  on opposition, 110
  taught law of Moses, 51
  taught plan of happiness, 35
Jacob's well, 102
James (Apostle), confronted cus-
    toms, 50
  "friendship of the world," 50
  on Gentiles, 51
  on prayer, 65
Jared, brother of. *See* Brother of
    Jared
Jarom, 51
Jensen family, 73
Jershon, 106
Jesus Christ, on allegiance, 55
  appeared in Kirtland Temple, 134
  appeared to Nephites, 51
  atonement of, 6, 7, 22, 35, 94,
    103, 105
  on charity, 18–19
  compassion of, 21
  crucifixion of, 42
  "even as I am," 58–59
  example of, 62–63
  faith in, 6, 21, 22, 82
  on forgiveness, 27–28
  fulfilled the plan, 7
  in Gethsemane, 65
  gives Sermon on the Mount, 8
  and healing, 105
  on the Holy Ghost, 63
  on ingratitude, 32
  intercessory prayer of, 58
  on law of Moses, 51
  on the learned, 23
  "learn of me," 103

on modern revelation, 64
on obedience, 32, 67
on the persecuted, 9
and the Pharisees, 43–44
and Pontius Pilate, 41–42
at premortal council, 6
on prophets, 68
provides comfort, 62, 66
relationship of, to Heavenly
    Father, 132, 139
and the rich young ruler, 46–47
and the Samaritan woman, 102
on service, 38
suffered, 106
on tradition, 48
Johnson, Sister, 115
John the Baptist, 135–37
  conferred the Priesthood, 134
John the Revelator, on love of the
    world, 49
Jones, Shavod, 31
Joppa, 52
Joshua, 43, 47, 78

— K —

Kimball, Spencer W., on diffusion
    of responsibility, 38
  on family prayer, 69–70
  on living with in-laws, 114
  on the scriptures, 64
  on service, 107
  on serving missions, 125
Kindness, 128
King Benjamin, on the Holy
    Ghost, 63
  on the natural man, 46, 57
  on obedience, 32
  on parenting, 120
  on service, 38
Kinship structures, 13
Kirtland Temple, 25, 134
Kleptomania, 107

Knudsen, Albert, 73–75
Korean War, 126–27
Korihor, 22
Kraus, Karl, 116
Kunze, Michael, 113
Kushner, Harold S., on dietary
     laws, 54
  on transmitting sins, 121

— L —

Laban, 81
Laman, 48, 65, 81
Lamanites, 21, 105–6
Lamoni, father of, 133
Landers, Ann, 103–4
Landfill (story), 30–31
Law of common consent. *See*
     Common consent, law of
Law of Moses, 50, 51, 137
Lawsuits, 31
LDS Social Services, 90
Learning, 22–24
Lee, Harold B., on confession, 91
  "constitution of the Church," 86
  on getting credit, 132
  on lifting others, 92
  "thick of thin things," 51
Lee, Harper, 36
Lee, Rex E., 141
Lehi, on agency, 35
  dream of, 42, 47, 50
  has vision of scriptures, 64
  on opposition, 5, 110
  sent for brass plates, 81
Lemuel, 48, 65
Levay, Sylvester, 113
Levin (fictional character), 39–40
Lewis, C. S., on "a living house,"
     138
Liberty Jail, 18
Ling, Murray, 69
Little red hen (fable), 37

Living waters, 102–3
Lucifer. *See* Satan
Luggage analogy, 75–76
Luttwak, Edward, *The Endangered
     American Dream,* 13

— M —

MacArthur, Douglas, 126–27
Macdonald, George, on "a living
     house," 138
Macomb County, Ala., 36
Magazines, pulp, 12, 13
"Make a Space for Joy" (poem), 84
Marriage, and agency, 110–12
  cultural traditions of, 50
  decision, 77, 97
  and ingratitude, 33–34
Mary (mother of Jesus), 136
Materialism, 16–17
Maxwell, Neal A., on academic
     scholarship, 22–23
  on opposition, 33
  on transmitting sins, 121
McConkie, Bruce R., on seal of
     Holy Ghost, 83
McCoy and Hatfield clans, 27
McDonald, Steven, 31–32
McKay, David O., on agency, 2
  "Every member a missionary," 38
  on spankings, 118–19
Melchizedek Priesthood. *See*
     Priesthood
Memories, long, 27
Mental illness, 87
Mercy, 21
Migraine headaches, 21
Milgram, Stanley, 96
Missionary responsibility, 125
Missionary Training Center, 142
Mocking, 42
Monson, Thomas S., on decisions,
     76–77

on gratitude, 34
Moral agency. *See* Agency
Mormon, on charity, 31
  on the Holy Ghost, 63
Mormon, Waters of, 85
Mormon Battalion, 83
Moroni, "come unto Christ," 107–8
  counseled by father, 31
  on spiritual gifts, 72
Moses, collected preliminary infor-
  mation, 78
  had clear vision, 77
  law of, 50, 51, 137
  restored priesthood keys, 134
Mothers, working, 16–17
Movies, 13
Music, 55–57
Music and the Spoken Word, on
  mental illness, 87
My Fair Lady (musical), 111

— N —

Name calling, 125
Napoleon, 24
National Football League, 80
Natural man, 39, 46, 57
Nauvoo exodus, 34, 82
Nauvoo Temple, 83
Nelson, Russell M., on accountabil-
  ity and choices, 9–10, 77, 84
  meaning of "peculiar," 58
Nephi, on the Holy Ghost, 63
  "liken all scripture unto us," 140
  obtained brass plates, 81–82
  on the scriptures, 64
  taught law of Moses, 51
Nephites, 21, 51, 58–59, 105–6
Netherlands, 106
Neustadt, Richard, 126–27
New England, 37
Newspaper columnists, 103–4

Nibley, Hugh, on rumor, 25
Nicodemus, 43, 47

— O —

Obedience, 32, 67, 120, 139
Oblonsky (fictional character), 49
Olson, Mancur, 37
Omner, 139
Opposition, 5, 18, 19, 21, 33, 110,
  111
Orchestra analogy, 116–17
Ordinances. *See* Priesthood
Oriental customs, 55
Orne, Martin T., on hypnosis, 101

— P —

Packer, Boyd K., on confession, 92
  on "counselitis," 98–99
  on ordinances, 68
  on support groups, 88
  on term "free agency," 6
  on wayward children, 122–23
Paranoia, 21, 33
Parents, 69–71
  and agency of children, 115–26
  and gratitude, 34
  interference of, 114–15
  promises to, 120–21
  and respectability, 44
Paris, Idaho, 141
Parked cars analogy, 11
Partridge, Edward, 134
Past, living in the, 39–40
Patience, 128
Patriarch (story), 71
Patriarchal blessings, 72
Patriotism, 55
Patterns, 90, 94, 95–96, 104–7
Paul (Apostle), angel appeared to,
  65

confronted customs, 50
conversion of, 137–38
"entertained angels unawares," 72
"examine yourselves," 90
"godly sorrow," 95
on the natural man, 46
"offspring of God," 36
"one in Christ Jesus," 57
"prisoner of Christ," 138
on the scriptures, 64
"wages of sin is death," 7
"ye are bought with a price," 7
Peculiar people, becoming a, 45–47
Peer pressure, 43
Perry, L. Tom, on obtaining brass
    plates, 81
Perry, Steven Kapp, 83
Persecution, 9, 58
Peter (Apostle), "be ready always,"
    142
    confronted customs, 50
    on Gentiles, 51
    has vision of unclean beasts,
        52–53
    "partakers of the divine nature,"
        46
    "a peculiar people," 45–46
Pharisees, 21–22, 43–44, 47
Philippines, 17
Phobias, 100
Physical appearance, 28–29
Physical punishment, 118–19
Pickering, Colonel, 111
Plan of happiness, 5, 7, 19, 35, 65,
    83, 110, 117
Polish customs, 55
Polly (musical), 83
Pondering, 80–81
Pontius Pilate, 41–42
Pornography, 12, 13–14
    letter of man addicted to, 13–14
Prayer, 65–66, 69–70, 99, 129

Premortal council, 4, 6, 123
Pride, 134–35
    See also Arrogance
Priesthood, Aaronic, 137
    ordinances, 15, 21, 67–68
    ordination to, 68
Privacy, 96
Prodigal (story), 14–15
Promiscuity, 48
Prophets, living, 68–69
Publicans, 44
Pulp magazines, 12, 13
Punishment, physical, 118–19
Purification, 34
Puyallup, Washington, stake con-
    ference, 34
Pyrenees, 24

— R —

Rebirth. *See* Conversion
Reconciliation, 9
Red hen (fable), 37
Relationships, family, 13
    marriage, 33–34
Repentance, 8, 9, 36, 90–91, 112
Respectability, and becoming a
    peculiar people, 45–47
    and cultural traditions, 48–59
    curse of, 41–59, 124–25
Responsibility, diffusion of, 38
    shifting, 35–39
Resurrection, 22
Retribution, 105
Revelation, 64, 68–69
    personal, 99
Revenge, 105
Rich, Charles C., 140–41
Richards, LeGrand, on maturing
    children, 117
Richards, Stephen L, on godly sor-
    row, 95

Rich young ruler, 46
Ricks College, 45
Righteousness, 8
Robinson, Robert, "Come, Thou
    Fount of Every Blessing," 143
Rocky Mountains, 82
Rodeo (story), 19–20
Romney, Marion G., on confession,
    91
    on offending the devil, 42
Rumor, 24–26

— S —

Sabbath, 43, 120
Sacrament, 68
Sacred Grove, 80
Samaritan woman, 102
Samson, 112
Samuel, 119
San Bernardino, Calif., 140
Sarcasm, 125
Satan, and compulsion, 112
    desires to derail youth, 11–12
    discourages repentance, 36
    and divisiveness, 58
    is master of deception, 11
    is waging war, 24
    offending, 42
    plan of, was rejected, 6
    and pornography, 13
    at premortal council, 4
    rages war on earth, 61–62
    and shifting blame, 35
    uses guerrilla warfare, 24
Saul. See Paul (Apostle)
Scholarship, 22–24
Schools, 38
Scott, Richard G., on healing, 104
Scriptures, 64
Self-awareness groups, 88–89, 93
    See also Support groups
Self-centered, 33
Self-confidence, 18

Self-esteem, 28, 92, 129
Sermon on the Mount, 8
Service, 38–39
    and healing, 107–8
Sexual abuse, 100–101
Shelem, mount, 80
Sherif, Muzafer, 96
Shooting victim (story), 31
Shopping, 110
Sins, accountability for, 35
    and agency, 7–9
    of commission, 36
    and happiness, 8
    of omission, 37
    private, 14
    transmitting, 121–22
Skipworth, Skippy, 74
Smith, Joseph, on forsaking family,
    55
    on happiness, 8
    on John the Baptist, 136
    on lying reports, 25
    on searching and pondering,
        80–81
    on tribulations, 18
    "trifle with the souls of men," 97
    was falsely accused, 26
    on wayward children, 122–23
Smoking. See Tobacco addiction
Soap operas, 12
Sorrow. See Godly sorrow
Spain, 24
Spanish hymnbook, 56
Spankings, 118–19
Special interest groups, 87–88
Spirit, the. See Holy Ghost
Stake missionaries, 75
Stakes, organizing of, 130
Stephen (Apostle), 137
Stephenson, Joan, on memory
    enhancement, 102
Stereotypes, 36
Sunday observance. See Sabbath
Support, sources of, 85–86

Support groups, 86–100
  and caveats, 88–89
  and confession, 90–94
  criteria for evaluating, 97–98
  and godly sorrow, 94–95
  and interviews, 95–97
  need for, 86–88
Symphony analogy, 116–17

— T —

Tabloids, 12
Tanner, N. Eldon, on interviews, 95
Tasmania, 69
Television, 12, 13, 18
Temple(s), blessings of, 55
  endowments, 15, 68, 142
  is greatest unifier, 59
  Kirtland, 25, 134
  Nauvoo, 83
Testimony, 62
T-form, 83
Therapy. *See* Counseling
Third World, 17
Time management filmstrip (story),
  28–29
Tobacco addiction, 12, 46, 54, 100
To Kill a Mockingbird (novel), 36
Tolerance, 128, 132
Tolstoy, Leo, *Anna Karenina*,
  39–40, 49
Traditions. *See* Cultural traditions
"Tragedy of the Commons, The"
  (treatise), 37–38
Translation of hymns, 56–57
Trauma, 27
Tribulations. *See* Opposition
Truman, Harry S, 126–27
Trust, in teachers, 103–4

— U —

Ulcers, 21
Unclaimed luggage analogy, 75–76

Unforgiving hearts, 26–32

— V —

Verdi, 56
Vernal, Utah, 83
Vienna, Austria, 113
Village green policy, 37
Visiting teaching, 75

— W —

Warfare, 24, 26
War in Heaven, 2, 6, 24, 61–62,
  89, 112
War on earth, 61–62
Wayward children, 122–23
Wealth, 45
"We Thank Thee, O God, for a
  Prophet" (hymn), 57
"Where's Your Luggage?" (news
  story), 75–76
Wimmer, Clifford, 34
Wine drinking, 46
Word of Wisdom, 54–55, 73
Wordsworth, William, on getting
  and spending, 17
Working mothers, 16–17
Worldliness, 16–17, 49–50
World War II, 56, 106
Wright, Orville and Wilbur, 117
Wyeth, John, "Come, Thou Fount
  of Every Blessing," 143

— Y —

Young, Brigham, on confession,
  90–91
  had clear vision, 77
  on parenting, 123

— Z —

Zarahemla, 105
Zechariah, on living waters, 102